BREAD FROM HEAVEN

BREAD FROM HEAVEN

Edited by
Paul Bernier, S.S.S.

PAULIST PRESS
New York/Ramsey/Toronto

Library of Congress
Catalog Card Number: 77-74581

ISBN: 0-8091-2029-1

Published by Paulist Press
Editorial Office: 1865 Broadway, New York, N.Y. 10023
Business Office: 545 Island Road, Ramsey, N.J. 07446

Printed and bound in the
United States of America

Contents

Introduction

Eucharistic theology has made tremendous progress since Vatican Council II. There has been greater development in two decades than occurred in the previous four centuries. Understandably so. Until recently, the manual tradition taught in our schools and seminaries was the direct result of Trent. And the vision of that Council was impaired by its struggle with the sacramental views of the reformers. We inherited a theology which was defensive and somewhat static. Like Trent, we continued to limit our theology to insistence on the real presence, the doctrine of the Mass as a sacrifice, and the notion of transubstantiation as a good theological explanation for the previous two realities. We were still defensive.

Vatican II, however, called for a "celebration" of the Eucharist. It spoke of it as a mystery to be lived, as a dynamic source of perfecting the Church, as resulting in works of charity, mutual help and missionary activity. The shift was on from a theology of confection to one of celebration. It is the presence of Christ throughout the entire liturgical action which gives the liturgy its value as an act of worship and sanctification. Hence the increased emphasis on the *quality* of participation and, indeed, on the whole life of the worshipping community. Eucharistic theology today, by returning to the sources, deepens our understanding of the sacred reality which is ours, roots us more deeply in salvation history, and challenges each of us to quicken our faith as did the first Christians.

The articles in this book were not chosen haphazardly. Rather, each of them was commissioned by EMMANUEL magazine in order to make a contribution to a more holistic and dynamic view of Eucharist. Hence there is a logical procession from a biblical view, through to how this mystery was understood in the early Church. This is followed by more modern theological reflections on the nature of Christ's eucharistic presence, and how this deepens our understanding of the theological virtues. Two final chapters challenge us once again to make the Eucharist a living reality in the secularized world of today. There is a common thread which joins all these chapters. It is a simple one, inspired by St. Paul's reminder in 1 Cor 11:28 that we must ever examine ourselves before eating the eucharistic bread. We are challenged throughout to reintegrate the Eucharist into our lives so that it goes beyond liturgy to become truly a mystery which is lived out daily, providing the force needed to change the world.

It is equally clear that the presentations are open-ended and that further reflection is not only invited but necessary. It might be interesting, for example, to study recent documents, such as the one on the non-ordination of women, in the light of the role of *faith* in effecting Christ's presence in the liturgy or the function of pastoral office in the Church. Likewise, after years of stress on the *ex opere operato* aspects of the sacraments, long overdue is the increased attention given here to the requirements on the part of the recipients for meaningful celebration.

Finally, the sacramental theology presented here is unabashedly dynamic. When we speak of sacramental change in the Eucharist, most people automatically think only of the bread and wine. The concept of Eucharist stressed here is that it is an assembling of a chosen people for an action, an action which is supposed to make a difference in their lives. The Eucharist has no meaning in isolation from the whole of life; participating in it (we used to say "assisting at" or "hearing" Mass) is no guarantee of growth in the Christ-life independently of the way the participants live their lives in the world. The history of the Eucharist and the very real place it had in the life of Jesus tell us we will never grow in union with Christ unless our lives become, like his, a response to the needs of others.

That is the real purpose of this book. It is addressed especially to those for whom the Eucharist is a familiar and frequent reality—and who, for that reason, can too easily reduce it to something to be reverenced or studied rather than lived. Theology, however, has ramifications for life. When Vatican II speaks of the Eucharist as the summit of Christian life to which all leads and from which all flows, it had in mind a profound change expected in all who shared the bread of Christ. For the bread that is shared joins us to Christ's own paschal mystery and implies an abiding and public commitment to alleviating the hungers of the human family. Christ's covenant is with all humankind, to whom we pledge solidarity each time we "examine ourselves" and eat the bread from heaven.

Paul J. Bernier, S.S.S.
EMMANUEL Magazine

Bread from Heaven

Edward J. Kilmartin, S.J.

The sixth chapter of the Fourth Gospel contains two miracle stories, a dialogue between Jesus and a crowd, and one between Jesus and his followers. This material has been arranged to convey one major affirmation which coincides with the purpose of this work announced in Jn 20:31: "These things have been written that you may believe that Jesus is the Christ, the Son of God, and that believing you may have life in his name."

In order to appreciate the structure of this chapter and the functions of each part, it is important to take account of what is stated near the end of the previous chapter. In Jn 5:36 Jesus affirms that "these very works which I am doing bear witness that the Father has sent me." In Jn 5:30-40 Jesus says that Scripture points to him and does not contain ultimate meaning in itself. Thus he rejects an interpretation of his works which is made by men and an interpretation of Scripture which derives from the past. Both his works and Scripture are testimony of the Father that he has "come in the Father's name" (5:43).

From this perspective the feeding miracle of Jn 6:1-13 is an example of how the works of Jesus witness to his mystery. John has recast the miracle of the multiplication of loaves and fishes found in the Synoptics in such a way that the center of attention is focused completely on Jesus. In the Synoptic accounts the disciples

1

take the initiative and distribute the food. In Jn 6:4 Jesus takes the initiative and even distributes the food himself (6:11)! Jesus is thus presented as one who knows men's hunger and personally feeds them. Moreover John also adds the account of the reaction of the crowd: a human interpretation of the meaning of the miracle. They see it as a sign that Jesus is the one sent from God to be a political Messiah (6:14). However, John observes that Jesus rejects this interpretation of his work and departs (6:15), and on the next day explains to them that the miracle is a sign of the "food which endures to eternal life, which the Son of Man will give you" (6:27).

The second miracle, the walking on the water, is also found in the Synoptics linked to the feeding miracle. But here again John's account is presented in a different way. Jesus' appearance to the disciples is described as an epiphany of the Son of God who immediately brings the disciples to a safe haven. Whereas in the Synoptics Jesus gets into the boat and goes with the disciples to the opposite shore, John's account gives the impression that Jesus did not enter the boat or that as he did so the boat reached shore: "And immediately the boat was at the land" (6:21). Thus Jesus' power is emphasized. This, together with Jesus' expression, "I am" (6:20), serves to concentrate the reader's attention on the mystery of Jesus. This expression is used by Yahweh to describe himself in the Old Testament. Thus the scene draws the attention of the reader to the correct interpretation of the miracle of the loaves and fishes. It points to the central theme of the discourse on the bread of life: Jesus is the Son of God, the unique mediator between God and man.

The dialogue between Jesus and the crowd on the

next day exemplifies how scriptural texts should be interpreted and so concretizes John 5:39-40. The crowd listened to Jesus exhorting them to seek the "food which endures to eternal life" (6:27). They also ask for a sign in order that they might believe that he can give them this food (6:30). Finally they ask for a sign comparable to the manna which the Israelites ate in the wilderness and quote the scriptural text which refers to this: "He gave them bread from heaven to eat" (6:31).

Jesus answers them by saying that this text of Scripture should not be interpreted as referring to the manna of the desert. The manna was only an external sign which points to the *true* bread which the Father gives. So "bread from heaven" refers to a bread which is neither manna nor the Torah: a bread which "gives life to the world" (6:33). The crowd accepts this interpretation: "Lord, give us this bread always" (6:34). Thus they admit that another interpretation of "bread from heaven" is possible besides manna and the Torah.

However Jesus goes on to say that he is the true bread: "I am the bread of life" (6:35). Thus he shows how a concrete scriptural text points to his mystery: a mystery which can only be accepted if the Father grants it (6:37).

This claim of Jesus is unacceptable to the Jews. If there is a "spiritual bread" outside the Torah it cannot be Jesus, "the son of Joseph" (6:41). Jesus answers by insisting that he is the bread of life (6:48) and consequently that "he who believes has eternal life" (6:47). Hence Jesus denies that because he is the son of Joseph it follows that he does not come down from heaven. Rather he affirms that in him the distinction between the external sphere of weakness of flesh and the spiritual sphere of God is over-reached; he is really the unique mediator between God and man.

This is the message of the discourse down to 6:50 which closes with a reference to the contrast between manna and the true bread of life. Those who ate manna died; those who eat the bread from heaven live.

Into this context the eucharistic passage is introduced (6:51-58). In 6:51c Jesus states: "The bread which I shall give for the life of the world is my flesh." The Jews do not respond with: "How can bread exist outside the Torah?" Rather they argue among themselves as to how Jesus, the son of Joseph, can be this spiritual bread (6:52).

In 6:53-58 the statement of 6:51c is elaborated. This passage focuses on the reality of Jesus in the flesh as source of life. It affirms that the encounter with Jesus in the flesh gives life and that apart from him this spiritual experience is not realized. But it does more than this! The use of eucharistic terminology allows for an unambiguous affirmation that Jesus is the Son of God who gives life. At the same time it affirms that even after death, Jesus "as flesh and blood" still remains source of life. It affirms that in the time of the Church Jesus, "as flesh and blood," is still the true bread of life. The historical Jesus does not merely point to the Son of God who is encountered in the Eucharist but is the Son of God so encountered. It affirms that to eat and drink in the Eucharist is not a spiritual experience apart from Jesus "as flesh and blood."

The remainder of the chapter records two different reactions to the teaching of Jesus about his mystery. One group of disciples reject it: "This is a hard saying; who can listen to it" (6:60)? Jesus responds that if his teaching offends them now, the scandal will be greater after his death (6:61-62). Then he goes on to contrast the view of his disciples with his own: "It is the Spirit that gives life; the flesh profits nothing; the words that I have spoken to you are spirit and life" (6:63). Equivalently he is saying: It is true, as you say, that life-giving belongs to the Spirit. Nevertheless I say to you that the words I, Jesus in the flesh, have spoken to you are of the Spirit and give life. The faithful disciple, Peter, says the same thing: "You have the words of eternal life" (6:68).

The Fourth Gospel was written in order that men might believe that Jesus Christ is the unique revealer of God's love for men and that believing in him as God's manifestation of love they might respond through love and so enter into the life of love of God. The response of faith is made in accepting Jesus' word as word of God (6:63; 8:56) and his person as Word of God. In the time of the Church the clearest affirmation of belief in the Incarnation—that Jesus in the flesh is not merely a unique messenger of God's revelation but actually the unique Son of God—takes place in the believing participation in the Eucharist. As act of faith, communion in the eucharistic flesh and blood is the most concentrated form of belief "that Jesus is the Messiah, the Son of God" (20:31).

Precisely because eucharistic communion is an act of faith, accepting God's love given in Jesus Christ for us to believe, it gives life. The nourishment provided by eucharistic communion is said to be "eternal life" (6:55). But what is eternal life? According to John 6:56 it involves a common life with Christ: "He who eats my flesh and drinks my blood abides in me and I in him." It involves a reciprocal interaction and interpenetration of Christ and the believer which touches life itself as the word "in" indicates. But what is eternal life? Ultimately the question is answered in John 6:57: "Just as the Father who has life sent me, and I live because of the Father, so the man who eats me will live because of me." The life shared is the life which Jesus has from the Father: divine life, a life which Jesus has from eternity (Jn 17:5) and which makes Jesus one with the Father.

We have seen that John 6 proclaims that Jesus in the flesh, during his earthly life, is the unique mediator between God and man. Furthermore it is also stated, through reference to the Eucharist, that Jesus in the flesh continues to be the unique mediator between God and man in the time of the Church. Finally it should be noted that several times in this chapter Jesus claims that he will raise up the believer on the last day (6:39, 40, 44, 54).

All these affirmations are contrary to the tenets of the heretics mentioned in the First Epistle of John. They held for a sharp distinction between the external and spiritual spheres: between "flesh" (man and his activity) and "spirit." In their view no interaction between the two spheres is possible. This means that man and his activity can only point to the spiritual sphere but never produce life-giving effects in the spiritual sphere. The precise view of these heretics is expressed in John 6:63: "It is the Spirit that gives life; the flesh profits nothing." The logical conclusion of this position is that "Jesus in the flesh" belongs to the ineffectual sphere of man and can only point in a vague way to the spiritual sphere of the Son of God but not *be* the Son of God. This view was actually articulated within the sphere of the Church of the First Epistle of John which is the same as the Church of the Fourth Gospel. Against this position 1 John 4:2 protests: "Jesus come in the flesh belongs to God." Again we read in this letter: "Jesus is the Son of God" (4:15).

Moreover these opponents understood that salvation comes through liberation from the flesh. They do not accept Jesus' resurrection in the flesh or the resurrection of the flesh in general. They oppose the perspective of John 6, wherein man must die, but since the life-giving activity of Jesus includes man's flesh he will rise. For John 6, on the Last Day a deep permanent union between flesh and spirit will be the lot of men. Thus the theme of resurrection, which is integral to the Fourth Gospel, stands over against the anthropology and soteriology of the opponents of the First Epistle of John.

With this background in mind, therefore, it is reasonable to suppose that John 6 was composed with an eye to the problem which existed for the Church of the Fourth Gospel: to refute heretics who were undermining faith in Jesus Christ, and the understanding of the full meaning of salvation.

Ignatius of Antioch's letters, written in the same milieu at the beginning of the second century, reflect the same situation. He says of heretics with whom he is acquainted: "They abstain from the Eucharist and prayer, because they do not confess that the Eucharist is the flesh of our Savior Jesus Christ. . . . It were better for them to have love, that they also may attain to the resurrection" (*Epistle to the Smyrneans* 7.1). Both John and Ignatius witness that the Eucharist is the test of belief in the Incarnation, proclamation of salvation of the whole man (flesh and spirit) and source of integration into the divine life in the time of the Church.

The Testament of Christ

Eugene A. LaVerdiere, S.S.S.

Every Christian is familiar with the Synoptic accounts of Jesus' Last Supper. Along with the Israelite Passover, no other meal in history has proven so decisive for so many people. From earliest Christian times, the Last Supper has been a primary source of liturgical expression, spiritual inspiration, communal self-understanding and theological reflection for all those engaged in the Way of the Lord. As such, it has marked Christian life as no other episode in Jesus' brief historical career save, of course, for his death to which the Last Supper is indissolubly linked in both history and tradition.

It is our purpose to examine Luke's account of this last of Jesus' meals with his disciples. By reflecting on the form of Luke's eucharistic institution narrative, we hope to shed fresh light on some of the less familiar but very significant aspects of our Last Supper heritage.

A Farewell Discourse

Luke 22:14-38 is cast in the form of a farewell discourse or testament of Jesus. Elements of a strictly narrative nature are minimal and secondary, completely relative to the words attributed to Jesus. In so composing the account of Jesus' Last Supper, the evangelist adopted a literary device which was already widespread in biblical and Jewish literature. The Book of Deuteronomy, for example, consists almost entirely of Moses' testament to the Israelites on the eve of his death as the latter prepared to enter the promised land. Especially noteworthy among Jewish antecedents are the *Testaments of the Twelve Patriarchs*, a second-century pre-Christian compilation which maintained its popularity and influence well into the New Testament era.

In the New Testament, the apocalyptic discourse of Mark 13 belongs to the same category, and both 2 Timothy and 2 Peter share many of its characteristics. A second Lukan farewell discourse may be found in Acts 20:18-35, Paul's parting testament to the Ephesian elders gathered at Miletus. And of course there is John 14—17, a literary unit which twenty centuries of Christian tradition have indissolubly associated with Jesus' last or farewell discourse.

Both Luke and John witness to an early Christian tendency to present the origins of the Eucharist as the testament of Jesus. This tendency, at first hardly perceptible save in relation to later developments, is already present in Mark's institution narrative (14:18-25) and its close Matthean parallel (26:21-29). In Mark and Matthew, however, the discourse elements remained implicit and undeveloped, severely limited to little more than the well-known liturgical formulas aptly described as eucharistic words of interpretation. Within the Synoptic tradition, it was left for Luke to exploit this literary potential and to give the embryonic discourse elements explicit form. Using traditional liturgical formulas as a nucleus and drawing on other ancient materials, he created the discourse presented in 22:14-38. Independently, John brought the eucharistic testament to its highest development in a discourse which comprises approximately one-fifth of his entire Gospel. Unlike Luke, his discourse does not include the liturgical formulas so firmly embedded in the Synoptic Gospel tradition.

The concrete source of the eucharistic discourse tradition lies not so much in the literary history of the New Testament as in the liturgical life and faith of the early Christians. From earliest times, the liturgical formulas utilized in the celebration of the Lord's Supper were attributed to Jesus himself. More specifically, they were referred to the last meal which Jesus celebrated with his disciples on the night before he died. From a formal point of view, this was indicated by providing the quoted words of Jesus with a third-person narrative framework. As is clearly attested by Paul in 1 Corinthians 11:23-25, the same historical setting and formal expression were retained in early Christian teaching concerning the Eucharist.

The early eucharistic liturgy's reference to Jesus' Last Supper reveals a keen sense of continuity with the historical life of Jesus on the part of his followers. It also points to an extremely important aspect of their belief concerning the nature of the Eucharist itself, namely, that the celebration of this meal actually effected the felt continuity. Gathered together for the breaking of bread, the early Christians were actually celebrating the Lord's Supper. This extremely realistic dimension of eucharistic faith was strongly emphasized by the liturgical words "Do this in memory of me," which were also attributed to Jesus.

The narrative framework which served to historicize the eucharistic formulas was highly adapted to the narrative form of the passion accounts and may well explain their inclusion in the Synoptic Gospels. It is their historical setting in Jesus' last hours, however, and the manner in which the celebration of the Eucharist joined the post-Easter community with Jesus' historical life which invited and facilitated Luke's presentation of eucharistic origins as Jesus' farewell discourse. In other words, Luke was able to develop a farewell eucharistic discourse or testament because *de facto* the early Christians actually saw the Eucharist as Jesus' testament to them. In 22:14-38, Luke merely translated into literary form what was already basic to Christian belief and self-understanding.

A Literary Hermeneutic

In ancient literature, a farewell discourse or testament was placed on the lips of a man about to die. Looking beyond his death to the life of his survivors and even to future generations, he speaks about various questions and issues yet to arise in the community which he is about to leave.

Literally, the testament represents a thrust toward immortality. In his effort to transcend the definitiveness of death and bypass the silence about to be imposed on him, a significant personage speaks a message to the future, giving his own earlier historically limited teaching an enduring quality.

Literarily, the testament represents the statement of a writer who looks back on a man's life with the conviction that death has not killed his message. It thus expresses the attitude of one who lives in a later age but who continues to identify with the dead man's life and attitudes. Time and events, however, had given rise to new situations which in many respects had dated the message in question. Continuity there was, but the lines of continuity had become uncomfortably taut. The dead man's message had to be re-expressed in terms of the new historical situation, else it would die. The testament is thus intended to bridge the temporal and experiential distance separating those who live in the present from a person with whom they stand in historical solidarity.

Historically, and from the point of view of later generations, the testament is an attempt to solve current problems or develop the attitudes needed to confront them by appealing to the recognized personal authority of one long dead and who can no longer be approached for guidance or solutions. The testament is accepted as authoritative to the extent that it both meets the needs of the present and resonates with the image and living memory of the person who speaks it.

Theologically, and in today's terminology, the testament can be called a hermeneutic. Its question, for example, is not "What *did* the message mean to the original hearers?" but "What *does* it mean to us?" Like the effort of the early Christians who applied the Old Testament Scriptures to the life of Christ, it applied the teaching of Jesus to a still later period of history. In form of presentation, the testamentary hermeneutic is literary and not expository or didactic such as is presupposed in texts like Luke 24:27, where Jesus is said to have interpreted all the Scriptures which applied to himself for the benefit of the disciples of Emmaus.

The Christological Context

Any consideration of our Last Supper heritage must pay close attention to its christological context. The ancient liturgical formulas and the various other sayings associated with them express or imply many christological judgments. These have been the subject of many well-known studies by both biblical scholars and theologians. As Ernst Kasemann indicated in his study of John 17, however, the very fact of attributing a eucharistic testament to Jesus is also an important christological issue, equally deserving of our attention.

The testament of Jesus is unlike that of any other man, because Jesus himself stands beyond all other men. Like Moses, Jesus lived and died; but unlike Moses, God raised Jesus to new life. The testament of Jesus expresses the faith of a writer and readers who experience the risen Jesus in their assembly for the breaking of bread. This fact profoundly affects the nature of Jesus' testament as given in Luke 22:14-38. For Luke and his readers, faith was expressed not only in the past tense of historical memory but in the present tense of vital relationships. It is this question which we must now explore.

Prescinding from the resurrection, we might express ourselves as follows. When Jesus died, he was somewhat over thirty years of age, being—so it was supposed—the son of Joseph . . . son of David . . . son of Abraham . . . son of Adam, son of God (cf. Lk 3:23-38). A poor man from Nazareth, he had lived as one of God's poor, responsive to every divine initiative, sharing his vision of God's reign and his own incarnation of that reign with a small number of disciples. Although he died a criminal's death, he had lived a just man's life, a life born of God.

Such a man does not die intestate. His bequest, however, does not lie in personally fashioned artifacts or in an accumulation of goods and properties, but in the impact of his life, spirit and teachings on all who had known him.

This alone would have sufficed to include Jesus

among the rare few whose lives become a legacy to every succeeding age of man. It could also account for any testament which would later be attributed to Jesus. Such a testament could then be numerically classed with those of other great religious figures. Differing in content, it would nevertheless share their same nature, being the testament of a biblical personage who died but whose message remained significant for future generations. Like the testament of Moses, it might also be considered as the very word of God.

The story of Jesus' life, however, did not end with his death. Severed from mortal life, he emerged into a new and transcendent life to be shared with all who gathered in his name. Death had not forever sealed Jesus' personal legacy to mankind. With the person of the risen Jesus, it broke the bounds of mortality to become the Life, the Spirit and the Way to God. Thus it is that Jesus' testament was nothing short of his own eternally living and life-giving self. Issued in the seventeenth or eighteenth year of the rule of Tiberius Caesar, when Pontius Pilate was procurator of Judea, during the high-priesthood of Annas and Caiaphas (cf. Lk 3:1-2), it abides in history as Jesus' metahistorical person extending sonship of God in word and sacrament to all who receive him.

The testament of Jesus is thus far from an ordinary bequest or last will. It is the living will of one who did indeed die but in dying became the Life. Against this christological background, why would Luke have attributed a testament to Jesus? The answer may be found in Luke's theology of history. More than any other evangelist, Luke was at pains to distinguish the historical life of Jesus from the period of his risen life with and in the community of his followers. In

Luke-Acts the two periods are literarily separated by the ascension accounts. Prior to his exodus (Lk 9:31), an event which began with Jesus' death and culminated in the ascension, Jesus was present through the ordinary modes of human communication. After his ascension, he could be recognized in the breaking of bread, but through an entirely new mode of presence which later generations would term sacramental. By highlighting the testament which Jesus disclosed to his disciples in the course of his last earthly meal, Luke thus emphasized the definitive nature of Jesus' death.

Jesus' testament is thus the final historical declaration of one who would henceforth be present in an entirely new manner. Addressed to those who continue to share in the Eucharist, it enabled the early Christians to interpret Jesus' on-going sacramental message in the language of the historical condition to which Jesus had once belonged and to which they continued to belong.

Jesus' Message to Future Generations

What then was Jesus' eucharistic message to the Church of the 80's and indirectly to all succeeding generations? What, in Luke's eyes, was Jesus' eucharistic legacy to Christian communities living in the absence of the historical Jesus? In the following paragraphs, we shall focus on what appear to be its principal features.

First, we note that the Eucharist is a meal (22:14) celebrated in Christ's memory (22:19). Theologically, its roots lie in a Passover meal long anticipated by Jesus in eager hope and celebrated in relation to his approaching passion and death (22:15). The Last Supper could thus be seen as the celebration of Jesus' passing into glory. The same eschatological context would continue to pervade the post-Easter actualization of the Lord's Supper which was celebrated as an effective sign of hope for men and women who would one day join the risen Lord in glory. Although the Christian Eucharist was not a yearly celebration of Passover, it quite obviously shared in the Passover significance of Jesus' Last Supper. Thus it is that the Eucharist has all the characteristics of an eschatological banquet in which the participants are oriented toward that final glory already fully enjoyed by Jesus.

Second, in a manner equaled only by John, Luke emphasized Jesus' presence in the celebration of the Eucharist. For Luke, be it noted, Jesus is present in the Eucharist primarily as a participant. At the Last Supper, he had presided over a meal in which he shared. Now that the Old Testament Passover and Jesus' own celebration of it has been fulfilled in the coming of God's reign (22:16, 18), he is once again in the midst of the community (22:27) joyfully gathered to share in a meal of fellowship. As the risen Lord, he continues to gather his disciples, to lead them in the prayers of blessing (22:17, 19-20) and to share in the community meal. Giving voice to the participants' faith in God, he enables his followers to appreciate their participation in a new covenant signified and effected in his own blood (22:20). Recalling that Jesus gave himself to the point of death (22:19-20), the Eucharist is meant to inspire and move the Christians to similar self-giving.

Third, the fellowship implied in the eucharistic gathering must be expressed in an attitude of *diakonia* or service. The importance given this theme (22:24-27) manifests the author's sensitivity to a growing problem in the community. We can only assume that some of the leaders of the community, and perhaps other members as well, had come to insist on their greatness. In their desire to be served at the eucharistic table, they had gradually assumed a position which might well have been acceptable in civil and political life (22:25), but which was completely out of keeping with the nature of the Eucharist (22:26). By his behavior at the Last Supper, Jesus himself had countered all such tendencies to social stratification. Drawing on a fragment of Jesus' teaching which previously had been associated with an entirely different context (cf. Mk 10:42-45; Mt 20:25-28), Luke applied Jesus' historical attitude to the situation now arisen.

Fourth, Jesus addresses himself to the danger of defection and to the need for loyalty in time of trial (22:21-23, 28, 31-34). The Christian community's problems in this regard had a special precedent in the behavior of Judas and Peter, but no one had escaped temptation (22:31). In the Jewish and early Christian context, the act of joining someone at table was an offer of *shalom* or peace, implying reconciliation, fellowship and solidarity. In such a context, Judas' betrayal stood out as an especially terrible act, clothed in hypocrisy. Betrayal by any future member of the community was equally reprehensible, directly contrary to the gesture posited by one who shared in the eucharistic meal. Denials there would be, but the community would never fail. Had not even Peter, who had three times denied knowing Jesus, returned to strengthen his brothers (22:32)?

Fifth, the loyal disciples who join Jesus in his kingdom eating and drinking at his table (22:30) are to continue his work (22:28, 30). In this they exercise the ruling role of service which Christ himself had received from his Father (22:29). In the exercise of their mission, they must provide themselves with those things needed for its fulfillment. During Jesus' lifetime, they had not been in need of money, traveling bag or sandals. Now, however, it was different (22:35-36). Luke was thus conscious of the need for adaptation to the new circumstances of a vastly expanded mission.

Such was Jesus' eucharistic message to Luke's readers. The problems on which it focused—namely, the nature and meaning of the post-Easter celebration of the Eucharist, the need for reassurance concerning Christ's presence, the redirecting of improper attitudes, the danger of defection and the place of continuity and adaptation in the Christian mission—would follow the Christian community on its long pilgrimage through history. So would Luke's creative interpretation of Jesus' response to these problems. Expressed with great sensitivity and with the loving care of one deeply involved in the eucharistic community, Luke's testament of Jesus comes to us as a classical expression of the nature and dimensions of eucharistic life. Its bold adaptation of tradition to current problems is a continuous challenge to all who are called to give new life to Jesus' undying words.

Give Us Each Day
Our Daily Bread

Eugene A. LaVerdiere, S.S.S.

In the words of Tertullian, the Lord's Prayer is a "resume of the entire Gospel." Set in the Gospel accounts of both Matthew (6:9-13) and Luke (11:2-4), this unique compendium of Christian spirituality has always been considered one of the high points in the teaching of Jesus.

Even if the prayer had not been recorded in our Gospel narratives, it would surely have survived as part of the Christian liturgical tradition, where it was included in the very earliest days of the eucharistic liturgy's formation. But then we might know the prayer only in its Matthean wording, which has dominated the life and prayer of the Church from the end of the first century. An expanded version of this same form is found in the *Didache* 8:2. Thanks to Luke, however, we also have the prayer in a second traditional form, which, at least with regard to the prayer's basic elements and original length, is more primitive than that of Matthew. Where the two texts parallel one another, however, Matthew and not Luke seems to have preserved the more ancient wording.

As our title indicates, our purpose in these pages is to concentrate on one single petition in the prayer's Lukan form: "Give (present imperative) us *each day* our daily bread." The Matthean form reads: "Give (aorist imperative) us *today* our daily bread."

Exegetes remain divided in their interpretation of this ancient Christian petition, whether in its present two forms or in the primitive nucleus from which they developed in the liturgical life of Jewish and Gentile Christian communities. Some, including Joachim Jeremias,[1] view the prayer as a request for eucharistic bread. Others, notably Henri Van den Bussche[2] and Heinz Schurmann,[3] advance non-eucharistic interpretations.

In the following pages, we shall propose a eucharistic understanding of our prayer for daily bread. In so doing, we shall be sensitive especially to the position of both the Lord's Prayer and the Eucharist in the socio-religious life of the primitive communities. We thus hope to build on the work of our predecessors by expanding the scope of the discussion beyond strictly historico-linguistic and literary considerations.

Bread

In ancient Palestine and elsewhere, whether in the Jewish or in the early Christian milieu, bread was the principal element of nourishment. Dipped into various sauces (Mk 14:20) and taken with other food such as fish (Jn 6:9), three small flat loaves provided an ample meal (Lk 11:5-6). Bread was such an important part of every meal that the term bread was frequently used in reference to the entire meal. Extending to everything one might eat on a given day, it applied even more generally to all that one needed for human sustenance. In the Lord's Prayer, bread thus includes all of our nourishment needs, bread itself as well as the other elements taken with it.

Bread was not viewed in abstraction from the human and religious context in which the meal was taken. It included the attitude of personal sharing and mutual presence as well as the implied pledge of continued solidarity and fellowship which characterized the meal. To the extent necessary, the meal was also a gesture of reconciliation. In this context, the participants were far more important than the food consumed. To share in a meal was to share one's very self. *Shalom* is the only word which aptly describes the ancient meal's social significance. Thus it is that our prayer for bread also addresses itself to the nourishment of human self-giving signified and effected by partaking of a meal.

Our Bread

There is something unusual about praying for "our bread." If the bread is ours, why need we pray for it? We might understand the request to mean that the things which are ours are given to us by God, thereby acknowledging the divine source of our sustenance and fellowship. We might also view it as a reference to bread which sons have a filial right to expect from their father. Such interpretations, and especially the second, may well be valid and contribute to a deeper understanding of the petition, but they also seem to fall short of the main point.

If the petition for bread is truly a prayer for nourishment and indeed for all the human values included in the meal, the pronoun "our" must refer to this entire setting. In a Jewish context, "our bread" would have referred to Jewish fellowship as expressed in a Jewish meal. In the Christian context, it obviously referred to the Christian meal and the specifically Christian attitudes it expressed. The prayer for "our bread" is thus a request for the bread which characterizes us, for the nourishment taken by Christians in social awareness of our identity as Christians.

This interpretation is supported by the very nature of the Lord's Prayer, which was a specifically Christian prayer, one which distinguished the disciples of Jesus first from those of John the Baptist (Lk 11:1) and later from rabbinical Judaism which formed around the synagogue and the Gentile pagans with whom they came in regular contact (Mt 6:7). Whether in the context of a sectarian prayer or in the Qaddish of the New Israel,[4] we would normally expect the prayer for bread to be for the nourishment enjoyed in distinctively Christian sharing. The expression "our bread" thus refers to the special meal of Christian fellowship; other nuances of the pronoun "our" must be judged secondary and in respect to their essential meaning.

Epiousios

In both the Jewish-Christian tradition of Matthew and the Gentile-Christian tradition of Luke, "our bread" is qualified as *epiousios*. Scholars do not agree on the interpretation of this term. It could even be that an adequate translation is impossible and that too precise a rendering is undesirable.

The word *epiousios* is not attested to in all of ancient Greek literature or even in the thousands of papyri which have done so much to clarify the Hellenistic vernacular of the first century. In the New Testament itself, the term appears exclusively in the two traditional texts of the Lord's Prayer. In other early Christian literature, it is found only in the *Didache*, which at this point reproduces the Matthean tradition, and in patristic works which quote or comment on the Lord's Prayer.

Since the Renaissance and the Reformation, modern translations have usually rendered the term by "daily" or its foreign linguistic equivalent. In this we recognize the preponderant authority of liturgical tradition, which preserved the Old Latin version's *panis quotidianus*. In other ancient versions, however, we read the equivalent of "continual" (Curetonian Old Syriac), "for our need" (Peshitta or Syriac Vulgate), and *supersubstantialis* (Latin Vulgate), which Jerome himself interpreted in light of the Gospel of the Nazarenes as "for tomorrow."

In a tradition long ago set by no less an authority than Origen, contemporary scholars have also proposed several etymological interpretations. The problem then becomes one of finding the correct Greek root from which the word is derived. Several possibilities have been advanced, yielding the meanings "necessary for existence," "for the current day," or "today," "for the following day," "for the future," the bread that "comes to" or "belongs to" today or to the "next" day.

In addition to ancient translations and etymological analysis, we might also examine similarly constructed words. As Origen indicated, the word *periousios* might well point us in the right direction. This term is used in the Septuagint exclusively in the expression "chosen" or "special people" (cf. Ex 19:5; 23:22; Dt 7:6; 14:2; 26:18). If this line of thinking were proven correct, the adjective *epiousios* would refer to the bread's special quality which is either superior or from above. This last interpretation would accord well with the meaning we have found in "our bread."

It is not our intention to pursue the above lines of research or argumentation. There is yet another approach, which to our knowledge all too easily escapes notice, perhaps because it is so very simple. As we indicated at the start of our discussion, the term *epiousios* appears only in the words of the Lord's Prayer. Seen in historical context, this fact itself is extremely significant.

We stand on solid ground in affirming that *epiousios* was a Christian neologism. If at some time the word had already been used in a manner which has left no literary or archaeological trace, there is very little likelihood that the Christians would have known of it, and from their point of view the term would still have to be considered a neologism. Further, since the word is common to both Matthew and Luke, its coining must have taken place at the earliest stages of the prayer's Greek formulation, prior to its separate development in the Jewish and Christian traditions quoted by Matthew and Luke. Finally, even if, as Joachim Jeremias argues, the term was intended as a translation of the earlier Aramaic word *mahar* meaning "for tomorrow," it still represented a Greek neologism, born of the creative impulse of the Greek-speaking community. First-century Greek offered a far more direct way of expressing "for tomorrow."

Why would the early Christians have coined a special word to describe "our bread"? The obvious reason is that they intended the word to describe a special reality, one which could not be adequately expressed by existing terms. Such a reality we know from the New Testament. It is the eucharistic bread or meal, the Christian meal of fellowship in which the participants shared in the risen life of Christ the Lord. No other reality corresponds both to the emphasis given this bread as *ours* and to the need to coin a new word to describe it. We must remember that in the extremely early days corresponding to the origins of the Lord's Prayer, there were as yet no universally established terms to refer to the Eucharist. Recognizing the uniqueness of their meal experience, the Christians needed a special word to refer to it. With no adequate term available to describe their distinctive meal, they had little choice but to coin one.

The subsequent development of a specifically Christian vocabulary to refer to "our daily bread" accounts for the early disappearance of the term *epiousios* from the language of Jesus' followers. The word's absence from the remainder of the New Testament can thus be accounted for in terms of the history of the Eucharist. On the other hand, its continuing presence in the Lord's Prayer provides a striking witness to the persistence of liturgical language. The variety of terms in the early versions of the New Testament indicates that in the ancient non-Greek Churches liturgical tradition referred to the reality encompassed by the word *epiousios* rather than to the word itself.

The term *epiousios* is thus more significant for the manner in which it evoked the eucharistic experience than for its conceptual content. Its precise etymology, which might well have posed a dilemma for the ancient philologist as well as for the modern, is of little import. By choosing different words, which for them referred to the Eucharist, the Syriac, Latin and other Churches brought out one or other aspect of "our daily (eucharistic) bread."

Our Daily Bread

In giving our Christian prayer for bread a eucharistic interpretation, two pitfalls must be carefully avoided. The first directly involves the Eucharist and the way we now experience it. The second concerns the Eucharist's relationship to other meals taken during the week.

When the first Christians prayed for their daily bread they had in mind an entire meal and not the small wafers or bread portions which have become typical of the eucharistic celebration today. They did have a term for pieces of eucharistic bread, *klasmata,* but in the early traditions the word referred to the broken elements left over from the celebration. In the accounts of Jesus' multiplication of loaves (Mk 6:43; 8:8, parallels, and Jn 6:13), the gathering of the *klasmata* emphasized the generous abundance of Christ's eucharistic nourishment; in terms of the actual celebration of the Eucharist, however, they were secondary.

Only late in the first century, when the term Eucharist itself came into use, did the *klasmata* refer to the broken elements blessed to be shared (*Didache* 9:3-4). In this case, "our daily bread" referred to a eucharistic situation similar to ours, in which the full eucharistic meal has been reduced to the two symbolic elements of bread and wine. This was hardly the case, however, at the time of the origins of the Lord's Prayer, when the bread and wine blessings represented two important moments in an entire meal. Even in the context

presupposed by the *Didache*, "our daily bread" referred
to a full meal, at least indirectly, since the bread used in
the Eucharist was identical to ordinary table bread and
readily evoked the values inherent in a meal.

In our own times, the symbolic and evocative value
of the bread and wine has largely been lost. As a result,
the Eucharist has become extremely spiritualized and a
eucharistic interpretation of the Lord's Prayer is open
to the criticism of undue spiritualization. This, however, is not the Eucharist as envisioned in the Lord's
Prayer, which represented adequate nourishment, both
physical and spiritual and in which a physical and genu-
inely human meal effectively symbolized the spiritual
and divine. The problem does not lie in the eucharistic
interpretation of the petition for our daily bread but in
the way we celebrate the Eucharist and the restricted
values it has come to represent.

The early Christians did not divorce their weekly
eucharistic meal from other meals shared during the
week. In addition to the sacramental continuity uniting
the physical and spiritual aspects of their weekly Eucharist, a second kind of continuity must be noted. The
weekly assembly on the first day of the week was the
Christian community's meal par excellence. As a meal
which gathered the entire Christian community as a
body, it nourished the attitudes of Christians who continued to be a Church even when they were not physi-
cally assembled. As the principal meal of the week, it
was related to other meals shared by smaller groups of
Christians united as a family or in the private gatherings of friends. For their part, all such meals evoked the
special meal of the entire community, which was each
one's principal meal of the week.

In every Christian meal, wherever two or three

were gathered in Christ's name (Mt 18:20), the Lord was present in a special way. Private meals differed from the community Eucharist in that they reflected and effected a unity narrower than that of the entire local community. They did not and could not replace the weekly gathering which expressed and developed that greater unity in Christ which transcends the blood ties of the human family and every social bond. In a limited sense, however, which Thomas Aquinas would have called participatory, every Christian meal can be called eucharistic. Unfortunately, most, or at least many, of our meals fail to qualify as Christian. Pastoral efforts aimed at remedying the meal's impoverished state in daily life would surely be well placed. They would enrich the weekly community liturgy and go a long way toward making it in fact the high point of the Christian week.

It is consequently false to oppose our prayer for eucharistic bread to the physical nourishment of daily sustenance. The weekly Eucharist was itself a physical nourishment, and it was continuous with the other meals taken by Christians during the week. As the principal Christian meal of the week, the former was certainly uppermost in the minds of those who petitioned God for our bread which is *epiousios*. Since all other meals were closely related to the weekly eucharistic meal of the entire community, however, the Christians equally prayed for all the nourishment, physical, personal and spiritual, which they required for their Christian growth and development.

Objectively, it might be quite accurate to translate "our daily bread" as "our eucharistic bread." Given present-day sociological realities, however, in which the celebration of the Eucharist remains abruptly cut off

from the remainder of the week, at least for most
Christians, in which most meals have become highly
depersonalized, and in which the Eucharist is hardly
perceived as a meal, even symbolically, it would appear
unwise to abandon the expression "our daily bread."
When we do speak of "our eucharistic bread" it must
be in terms of the ideal of eucharistic renewal for which
all yearn.

Give

Everything we have considered up to this point
serves to define and qualify the request which is essentially worded in the verb "give." In so turning to God,
the early Christians affirmed their dependence on God
for bread. They also manifested their faith in God and
confident trust that he could give this bread and that as
their Father he would actually do so. The petition thus
expresses our precise personal relationship to God, who
is the source and giver of human sustenance.

The use of the particular verb "give" cannot have
been accidental. This same verb, which is found in both
the Matthean and the Lukan versions of the Lord's
Prayer, was also closely associated with bread in the
earliest liturgical texts and other eucharistic narratives
which referred to Jesus' action at the Last Supper: "He
took *bread* . . . and *gave it* to them."

In Jesus' farewell discourse, Luke developed the
relationship between Jesus' own giving action and that
of his Father: "I for my part assign to you the domin-
ion my Father assigned to me. In my kingdom you will
eat and drink at my table" (Lk 22:29-30). In this, Luke
reflects the traditional faith that the bread partaken at

Jesus' table continues to be given by his Father to the Christians who sacramentally provide human expression to the Lord's on-going role in history. We can then understand why the early Christians turned to the Father in their request for eucharistic bread. In the following of Christ, they were praying in the manner which Jesus himself had introduced when he addressed God as *Abba* (O Father).

Luke's use of the present imperative of the verb "give" contrasts with Matthew's aorist imperative. The latter indicates a single act; the former, repeated action: "keep giving," "give over and over again." This attitude is altogether consistent with the general tendencies manifested in Luke-Acts. Its presence in the Lord's Prayer, however, indicates that the same attitude was generalized in the Christian communities from which Luke drew his inspiration.

Give Us

The first person pronoun, which is the indirect object of the verb "give," appears in the plural. The early Christians did not pray that our Father give each one his daily bread but that he give them their daily bread. This plural form was essential to the nature of the petition. It reflects the great social awareness of the early Christian community. Like the people of the old covenant, they saw their relationship to God as realized in and through the new covenant community. The individual Christian's well-being was inseparable from that of the community to which he belonged.

Although the first person plural was characteristic of all Christian prayer, at least indirectly,[5] its most significant use was in the request for Christian nourishment. Since the eucharistic meal was intrinsically a social event, a prayer cast in the first person singular would have been completely out of character with the ecclesial nature of our daily bread and the sharing of self which it both called for and expressed.

Thus it is that praying that our Father give us our daily bread places special emphasis on the selfless fellowship intrinsic to every genuine celebration of the Eucharist. Called to love his neighbor as indeed he loves himself, the Christian realizes his own well-being by reaching out to others. Self-love and personal interest are fulfilled by selflessly loving those who manifest their solidarity in eucharistic sharing. Further, love must even reach out to all who are called to the Eucharist but for some reason do not respond. The prayer for "us" includes not only all who have responded but more broadly all who are called.

Each Day

The expression "each day" appears only in Luke's version of the Lord's Prayer. While Matthew's "today" focuses more explicitly on the Christian's absolute trust that God will provide for the morrow, Luke looks to the on-going process of life. The prayer's temporal qualifier "each day" is thus an excellent correlative for the present imperative "give," which had already called for repeated action. Committing himself to the future, the Christian recognizes that life's continuation depends on his Father.

The words "each day" also said a great deal about how the suppliants viewed themselves. Of its very na-

ture, prayer is an acknowledgment of human need. By
praying that bread be given each day, the early Christians may have had a very concrete social image in
mind. They compared their position before God to that
of Jerusalem's poor who depended on the community's
generosity for the daily distribution corresponding to
each one's needs (Acts 2:45; 4:35; 6:1). Just as community solidarity and *koinonia* was the basis for sharing
with the poor, in the same way God's fatherly solidarity
with the family of Christians provided the basis for
their petition and its daily fulfillment.

The expression may also have been a reference to
the bread of each day which God had given the Israelites in the Exodus. In Exodus 16:4-5 (Septuagint), the
manna is explicitly given as a bread from heaven which
God gives to his people each day. The Christian's need
for each day was thus viewed as that of a liberated people journeying as God's poor through life's purifying
desert on the way to the kingdom of promise.

As a comprehensive expression of Christian needs,
our prayer for bread is a resumé within a "resumé of
the entire Gospel." Economically phrased, it leaves
nothing unsaid. The full intent of so generic a statement, however, could not possibly be consciously advert-
ed to in every act of prayer. Such is the religious genius
of a truly universal and classical prayer, which is suited
to the personal life situation of every Christian. Its precise content must be spelled out by the process of history, by personal and community maturation and by the
specific needs of the moment. Focused on the Eucharist
as the most characteristic and pervasive need of the
Christian community, the prayer invites all of us to
direct our lives in a eucharistic ambience.

NOTES

1. J. Jeremias, *The Lord's Prayer* (Philadelphia, Fortress Press, 1964), pp. 23-27.

2. H. Van den Bussche, *Understanding the Lord's Prayer* (New York, Sheed and Ward, 1963), pp. 109-118.

3. H. Schurmann, *Praying with Christ* (New York, Herder and Herder, 1964), pp. 55-64.

4. Not only are several elements of the Lord's Prayer drawn from the Jewish prayer known as the Qaddish, but the Lord's Prayer actually replaced the Qaddish in the life of Jewish-Christian communities once they had been expelled from the synagogue. Since the prayer is included in the Matthean effort to reformulate Christian identity in terms of a New Israel, it appears entirely appropriate to view the Lord's Prayer as the Qaddish of the New Israel at least at this point in early Christian history.

5. The community consciousness of early Christian prayer was developed by the author in *Trumpets of Beaten Metal* (Collegeville, The Liturgical Press, 1974), pp. 80-92.

Eucharist and Community

Edward J. Kilmartin, S.J.

Christians believe that the Risen Lord is the source of their union with God and of union among themselves. This belief is announced in the common confession that "Jesus is Lord" (1 Cor 12:3) and more profoundly by the celebration of the Lord's Supper.

Since Christian faith tends to, and finds its fullest expression in, the eucharistic celebration, we can also say that the Christian community most perfectly manifests itself and so realizes itself in the Eucharist. As the most concentrated expression of the mystery of the Church, the Lord's Supper serves as a norm for judging everything else in the Church. Whatever exists in the concrete daily life of the Christian community and is not in harmony with the Eucharist must be judged as both obstructing the manifestation of Church and preventing the building up of the Church as body of Christ. Reciprocally, the celebration of the Eucharist reveals and contributes to the growth of the body of Christ in the measure that the community is not a foreign body but truly the body of Christ.

The Apostle Paul has something to say about this relationship of Church to Eucharist. His remarks in 1 Corinthians 10:14-33 and 1 Corinthians 11:17-34 can be subsumed under the theme: Eucharist and Community.

34

1 Corinthians 11:17-34

In this pericope Paul treats of one aspect of the basic concern of this epistle: the unity of the community. He underscores one of the causes of disunity: an abuse at the Lord's Supper. He exposes the abuse (17:22), evaluates it in the light of the meaning of the Eucharist and offers practical advice for avoiding the judgment of God and the social abuse (23-33).

The factions which exist at Corinth are revealed by the way the assembly conducts itself at the Lord's Supper: there is no eating together and no sharing of food and drink with the poor. Paul judges that this fostering of factions by the insensitivity to the demands of unity in Christ is sinful and so makes the "coming together" unprofitable (17). The meal is a caricature of the Lord's Supper (20). The selfish conduct of some is also labeled as a despising of the Church of God and a shaming of the poor (22).

We may assume that the rich at Corinth, in the matter of social demands, made a complete distinction between the meal of satiation and the celebration of the memorial of the Lord which followed. They joined the poor for the latter activity which they considered to be spiritually profitable. Paul, however, sees an intimate relationship between the two activities. He is not concerned directly with the excessive drinking as improper at the Lord's Supper. He is not even concerned directly with the general requirement of the rich to contribute to the needs of the hungry poor. He is concerned rather that the community meet together as one family and share their food and drink as a natural expression of the love they have for one another.

For Paul the lack of love, manifested by each one going "ahead with his own meal" (21), threatens the reality of the Eucharist. He is not accustomed, as we are, to make a distinction between a valid and a fruitful Eucharist. His preoccupation is with what actually happens to the community as a result of their meeting together. The Lord's Supper should be a spiritually profitable event. Hence he can say without qualification: "When you meet together (understood: as you are accustomed to do), it is not the Lord's Supper that you eat" (20). As Paul views it, the outward accomplishment of the memorial of the Lord is not sufficient to realize the Lord's Supper in truth. It is, therefore, a Pauline principle that where the community dimension is deficient the Lord's Supper is not fully realized.

This view of Paul is in harmony with Matthew 5:23. The poor at Corinth had something *against* the rich who shamed them (22). Hence unless the rich rectified this situation the Lord's Supper was not beneficial for them. Paul's understanding of the Eucharist is in keeping with the New Testament tradition which relates the service of brotherly love to the Eucharist (Lk 22:26-27; Jn 13:1-20). In contrast to this, the rich viewed participation in the Eucharist as involving the individual's relation to the Risen Lord in an exclusive sense. They saw no problem in associating with the poor only for the rite of the bread and cup. Paul rejects this. The "coming together" (17, 18, 33, 34) must be such that the community finds itself really together before engaging in Christian worship together.

It is noteworthy that Paul speaks of the conduct of the rich not only as a shaming of the poor but also as a despising of "the Church of God" (22). Probably "Church of God" refers to the community of God in a more inclusive sense (= the whole community of believers living in union with God and with one another). If so, this despising would consist in preventing the Church from being manifested and realized in this concrete community. This despising of the Church of God is ultimately a despising of God himself who has established the Church through Christ. Hence Paul can speak, in v. 29, of the judgment of God on the unworthy participants of the Lord's Supper.

Up to this point Paul has called attention to the requirement of brotherly love in order that the Church might be truly present, manifested and so grow in Christ through the celebration of its faith. He could have added, along the line of Galatians 5:13-15, a simple exhortation to the rich to recognize that their freedom in Christ is not for self-indulgence but for love and concluded with the pastoral advice of vv. 33-34. But he does not choose this approach nor does he appeal to the obvious function of a communal meal to manifest and support fellowship. Rather he introduces, in rather abrupt fashion, the narrative of the institution of the Eucharist (23-25) and then criticizes the abuse in the light of this tradition received "from the Lord" (23). He does so because of his understanding of the relation between Eucharist and Church which is expressed in the account of institution used in the Corinthian community.

Among the more notable differences between this account and that of the Gospel of Mark, the most important is the formulation of the words spoken over the cup. In the case of Mark 14:24 the gift of the cup is the blood of Christ qualified as blood of the covenant: "This is my blood of the covenant." In 1 Corinthians 11:25 the gift of the cup is affirmed to be the "new cov-

enant," while the blood of Christ is seen to be the
means of establishing the new covenant. "This cup is
the new covenant in my blood" means that the new
covenant is mediated by the gift of the cup (= the blood
of Christ, as 1 Corinthians 10:16a states) in virtue of
the redemptive death of Jesus (= in my blood; in the
power of my death).

The reference to the *new* covenant relates the gift
of the cup to Jeremiah 31:31, where the "new covenant" is described as something different from that originally given to Israel. This new covenant is written "in
the heart" (Jer 31:33). It thus gives true knowledge of
God and the ability for proper relations between God
and mankind and between men themselves. For Paul
the new covenant, the new order of salvation, the gift
bestowed through the sharing of the eucharistic cup, is
an interior grace. It is the dynamic principle of Christian life, the life of faith, which expresses itself in the
service of God, the community of believers and the rest
of the "many" for whom Christ died. Thus the abuse at
the Corinthian meal is contrary to the gift bestowed
through the cup which gives the ability to live a life of
freedom *from* selfish interests and *for* the service of one
another in Christ.

In the light of this consideration it becomes under-
standable why Paul would appeal to the account of institution of the Eucharist to correct the abuse of the assembly. We can also come to a better appreciation of
the import of Paul's statement in v. 26: "For as often
as you eat this bread and drink this cup, you proclaim
the death of the Lord until he comes."

Paul is talking about a proclamation of Jesus'
death as redemptive. For Paul such a proclamation is
not made by the merely external eating and drinking of

the Lord's body and blood. It takes place ultimately through the visible effects which Jesus' victorious death has on the community of believers. In the measure that the community lives in union with one another in love, it is a concrete proclamation of the redemptive death of Jesus. The members show by their lives that Jesus' death is redemptive now, that it heals the divisions of mankind brought about by sin.

In v. 26 Paul seems to be talking about the ideal participation in the Eucharist: one in which the community dies to selfishness, lives a life of love and so proclaims the death of the Lord. This verse, it seems, should be understood as an exhortation: "As often as you eat this bread and drink this cup, you ought to proclaim the death of the Lord by *dying to self*," a thing which some are not doing since they foster factions in the very celebration of the Lord's Supper.

This interpretation makes clear why Paul can conclude in v. 27 that the unworthiness of some participants, derived from their personal failure to proclaim the death of the Lord by dying to self at the Lord's Supper, is also a sin against the eucharistic Christ who lived and died for the "many" and gives believers the power to do likewise.

Paul goes on to give pastoral advice. He advocates self-judgment as a preparation for sharing in the Lord's Supper (28). This self-assessment, in the context of the passage, must take into account one's conduct at the meal. Is it consistent with the mystery of the body of Christ? One must, so says v. 29, "discern the body," i.e., judge correctly concerning the body, lest one eat and drink a judgment upon himself. The phrase "not discerning the body" or "not regarding the body in its peculiarity" could refer to the eucharistic body in its

specific claim to fraternal love. On the other hand, it
could refer to both the eucharistic and ecclesial body,
and so mean: not recognizing the unity of the ecclesial
body effected by the eucharistic Christ (cf. 1 Cor 10:16-
17) and demanded by the eucharistic Christ.

The passage closes with pastoral advice: self-judgment in humility will avert the judgment of God (31);
the social abuse will be remedied by waiting for all to
assemble before eating (33).

1 Corinthians 10:14-33

In this chapter Paul develops a theme which is
expressed in the last sentence of the preceding one: it is
not enough to preach to others; true Christian ascet-
icism must be practiced if one is to be saved (9:27). He
begins by pointing out that the sharing in the deliverance from Egypt and the "spiritual food and . . . spiritual drink" did not suffice to assure the Israelites of
salvation (1-6). There remained the duty of conformity
to the will of God. Paul says that this should serve as a
lesson for the Corinthians (6, 11). Here Paul implies
that the sharing in Baptism and the Eucharist without a
life conformed to the Gospel does not guarantee salvation.

In vv. 14-33 Paul takes up a concrete application
of the principle advanced in vv. 1-13: the necessity of
conforming one's life to the Gospel. He returns to the
problem of eating meat derived from heathen sacrificial
rites. Previously in this epistle he implied that this meat
can be eaten provided that no scandal was given (1 Cor
8:1-13). However, in that passage he cautioned against
the practice of participating in banquets in pagan tem-

ples even by knowledgeable Christians. While they did not consider that this involved them in the worship of idols or that it was spiritually profitable, the less knowledgeable could be led by their example to conclude that it was spiritually beneficial.

Now Paul again addresses the question of eating meat with unbelievers at a banquet in a pagan temple. He has just been talking about "temptation" (13). Hence the exclamation "Shun the worship of idols" (14) should be understood as: Flee from situations in which worship is being offered to idols, for it will be the occasion of sinning. Why? The reason is given in vv. 19-20: Such worship is inspired by demons and so results in partnership with demons.

But in what does this partnership with demons consist? The knowledgeable Christians do not admit that idols have any real existence or that eating of meat derived from heathen sacrificial rites is spiritually profitable. They do not experience that they are drawn into the worship of idols by sharing a banquet in a pagan temple. Is Paul warning them, nevertheless, that they will ultimately be drawn to the worship of idols by demons who inspire such worship, who influence the participants, by their presence, to judge such worship as beneficial? This is possible. However another interpretation, which can show a connection between vv. 14-22 and 23-33, seems preferable.

In vv. 23ff. Paul affirms what is implied in 1 Cor 8:1-13: meat derived from pagan sacrifices can be eaten provided it causes no scandal. It is allowable because it is the Lord's food (26). Still Paul insists that it must be taken with *thanksgiving* (30). Consequently, partnership with demons appears to consist in giving scandal to those who see the knowledgeable sharing in the table of demons. This is the same thing as not giving thanks to God. It is doing the work of demons.

The concrete way that thanksgiving to God is shown consists in not seeking one's own good "but the good of the neighbor" (24), i.e., by eating sacrificial meat in such a way that others are not scandalized and come to think it is spiritually profitable (28-29; cf. 1 Cor 8:8-13).

The conclusion of the pericope supports this interpretation. In v. 31 Paul says: "So, whether you eat or drink, or whatever you do, do all for the glory of God." Concretely this means, as v. 33 states, seeking to contribute to the good of the "many, that they may be saved." Hence in the matter of eating sacrificial meat, one must not give offense "to Jews, Greeks or to the Church of God" (32).

How does 1 Corinthians 10:16-17 fit into this context? Paul compares the Lord's Supper to the Hebrew communion sacrifice (18). The Jews know what communion sacrifice means: those who eat the sacrifice are partners in the altar. If they see Christians participating in heathen communion sacrifices they will be scandalized. Hence the reference to giving no offense to Jews (32). However, the whole weight is placed on a comparison between the Eucharist and heathen communion sacrifice: the Eucharist is contrasted with the table of demons (21).

In 1 Corinthians 10:16, a formula known to the Corinthians (as the rhetorical question indicates), the cup is said to afford a participation in the blood of Christ and the bread a participation in the body of Christ. The rite of the bread and cup is understood to mediate the saving presence of the Risen Lord to the communicants. In v. 17 Paul gives a commentary on the significance of the sharing in the body of Christ. The movement of this verse operates from the thought of *unity*: the bread is one (17a); the many partake of the one bread (17c); all are one body (17b). In effect, Paul teaches that Christians are one in Christ through eucharistic communion. Commenting on this verse R. Bultmann says: "The unity of the community can only be based on the unity of the bread, if the bread (as v. 16b states) is the body of Christ" (*Theology of the New Testament* I, p. 145).

   This verse is important for the argument of the whole passage. Paul is saying that because Christians are one in Christ through the Eucharist, they are called to the ethical demands expressed in vv. 23-29. They must do the work of their one Lord and not the work of demons. In the Eucharist, as vv. 16-17 state, Christ is affirmed to be the one Lord of the community to which he unites himself. It follows that the participants must conform themselves to the will of the one Lord: take seriously the unity of believers in Christ effected by the Eucharist. They must seek the neighbor's good above personal benefits (23-29). In contrast to this, participation in the table of demons, in such a way as to give scandal and not build up the Church, means to serve other lords and will provoke "the Lord to jealousy" (22). And this seeking the neighbor's good has reference also to the Jews and heathens (32), who are among the many whom the Lord wishes to save (33).

Summary

   In 1 Corinthians 10:14-33 Paul deals with the problem of eating meat derived from heathen sacrifices.

He approaches the question from the viewpoint of the implications of the Lord's Supper. Through the eating of the bread and drinking the cup Christians are united to their Lord and this implies unity among themselves. Consequently they must seek to fulfill the will of the one Lord: seeking the good of the neighbor, eating and drinking, and doing all else in such a way as not to give scandal. To act otherwise is to serve other lords.

Paul stresses the cleanness of food taken with thanksgiving, i.e., in such a way that the neighbor is not scandalized. By so acting one is conformed to the meaning of the Eucharist: the sharing in the one Lord means to accept him as Lord and seek to fulfill his will by working for the salvation of the "many."

The movement of 1 Corinthians 11:17-34 is somewhat the same. Selfishness at the Lord's Supper is an offense against the eucharistic Christ because it works against the unity effected by Christ. The remedy is self-examination which leads to the subjective proclamation of the death of the Lord, i.e., dying to self in accord with the meaning of Christ's death.

Paul views the Eucharist as making demands on the social and moral behavior of the community. He also understands that the sharing in the eucharistic Christ in faith creates the unity of all in Christ and so gives the power to meet the ethical demands of the Gospel.

Feed My Sheep: Eucharistic Tradition in Mark 6:34-44

Eugene A. LaVerdiere, S.S.S.

Many years, decades actually, before Mark's creation of the first literary Gospel, traditional stories of Jesus' miraculous feeding of a vast crowd circulated wherever the Gospel word took root. As a favorite Christian story, the event lived and developed, reflecting the general lines of emergent Christian culture, if such it can be called, as well as a multiplicity of local concerns. Eventually, some of those traditional accounts found a more permanent home in the New Testament.

Indeed the story of the multiplication of loaves and fishes was so rich that it was included in all four of our classical Gospel narratives. Mark, and Matthew after him, went so far as to present two distinct traditions of the same event, one Jewish-Christian (Mk 6:34-44; Mt 14:13-21), the other Gentile-Christian (Mk 8:1-9; Mt 15:32-38). In his account, Luke was particularly conscious of the urban context of his readers (9:10-17), and John was careful to situate the event among the signs which prepared for Jesus' discourse on the bread of life (6:1-13).

Since each telling of the event not only transmitted earlier traditions, but reflected changing liturgical practices and expressed the pastoral intentions of the evan-

45

gelists, the phenomenon of multiple literary attestation makes of the account an extremely precious witness to the historical development of early Christianity. The eucharistic nature of these texts enables us to see the Eucharist's intimate relationship to the total life of the Church.

It is not my purpose to explore the literary history of the six accounts now contained in the New Testament or to conduct a minute analysis of their formal, structural or linguistic similarities and differences. Nor do I intend to trace the biblical lineage of all the words and expressions found therein. Tempting as such studies may appear, I have set on a more modest course, limiting my essay to a number of observations concerning the development of the tradition which underlies Mark 6:34-44. Obviously, to do this effectively, I shall frequently have to consider the entire range of New Testament multiplication stories.

The Event

It all began with an event. A large crowd of Galilean men and women had been following Jesus for some time. Attentive to his words and unmindful of their own physical needs, they found themselves in a place unable to provide for their nourishment. Somehow, contrary to all expectations, food was amply supplied. The event evoked wonder on the part of those who shared in the unexpected bread and fish that day. God had acted on their behalf! Already nourished by Jesus' word, the disciples, and no doubt, many in the crowd, credited God's action to Jesus' powerful intervention.

Further precision is extremely difficult in describing the event, and it may be that even in the above nuanced statement we have passed beyond the limits set by rigorous criticism. The extant traditions are not consistent on the number of people involved, on the precise roles of Jesus and the disciples, on the place where the event occurred, on the quantity of food available and on the amount gathered after the meal. We may assume that even the first accounts differed in their presentation and that various groups of Christians situated the story, perhaps quite unconsciously, in a cadre which was familiar to them. We can understand this tendency to supply details from the way we Westerners speak of the apple in Eden, while many Africans refer to a banana and Near Easterners spontaneously think of a fig or pomegranate. In actual fact, Genesis does not indicate the nature of the fruit. Many later precisions, of course, reflect a conscious choice of biblically pregnant words and phrases.

As the story reaches us, the original contours of the event are largely obscured by the rich liturgical and theological reflection which accompanied and spurred its transmission. Whatever did actually happen on that day in Galilee, however, clearly invited the interpretations which would be given it. The Gospels do not present unfounded faith interpretations or imaginative value statements detached from their moorings in Jesus' life; they give us events as interpreted and responded to in faith. Rather than mourn over our inability to circumscribe the event after the manner of modern history, we should rejoice in the multiple interpretations to which it was open and which have assured its enduring significance. We stand enriched, not impoverished, by the text's present biblico-literary presentation.

Basic Insights

If the feeding event was preserved and transmitted in the early Christian communities, it must be that it not only said something about an extraordinary incident in the remote origins of Christianity but continued to speak to Christians in the new situations which arose after the death-resurrection of Christ. Faith-insight linked the episode especially to the communities' eucharistic meals and to the nature and purpose of the Church's life and mission in the world.

The Eucharist. At an extremely early date in the history of tradition, the multiplication of loaves was presented as a eucharistic event. Accordingly, the text of Mark 6:34-44 is full of eucharistic implications. Most striking is the reference to the ancient liturgical formula introducing Jesus' eucharistic words: "Then taking the five loaves and the two fish, Jesus raised his eyes to heaven, pronounced a blessing, broke the loaves, and gave them to the disciples to distribute" (v. 41). Although the formula's wording has been adapted to the narrative context of the multiplication, its scarcely veiled presence is unmistakable.

A similar statement is found in each of the New Testament narratives of Jesus' miraculous feeding. The eucharistic interpretation of the incident must consequently stem from the earliest stages of the tradition's formation, prior to its bifurcation into the Synoptic and Johannine branches of tradition or any other development which came to be distinguished from the primitive root tradition. Otherwise we would expect to find the reference to the liturgical text absent from at least one of the texts and especially from John who did not include the words of eucharistic interpretation in his account of Jesus' Last Supper.

That the Eucharist remained a constant factor in the development of the text can be seen not only from the adaptation of the liturgical formula to prevalent local practices but also from the gradual removal of the fish from the core of the story as the tradition continued to develop. In this respect we might compare Mark 6:34-44 with 8:1-9. We note that in this Gentile-Christian tradition, mention of fish has disappeared from the bread formula: "Taking the seven loaves he gave thanks, broke them, and gave them to his disciples to distribute" (8:6). Nor had fish been mentioned earlier as they were in 6:38. Instead they enter the narrative as a kind of postscript: "They also had a few small fish; asking a blessing on the fish, he told them to distribute these also" (8:7). Unlike Mark 6:43, Mark 8:8 does not mention fish among the leftovers.

With one minor difference, the same phenomena may be observed in John 6:9-13. Although fish had been indicated as part of the available fare (6:9), they are not included in the liturgical statement concerning the bread (6:11a) or among the leftovers (6:12-13). As in Mark 6:41b, they are included as a postscript, demonstrating fidelity to earlier practice as well as to the original event.

These literary differences are not accidental. They reflect a development of eucharistic practice in which the Eucharist no longer consisted in a full meal but had been limited to the primary elements of a symbolic meal. Earlier, when the more primitive eucharistic practice still obtained, the Christians saw no problem in mentioning fish along with bread. The concrete equation between the multiplication event and the early Eucharist allowed for a comfortable mention of the fish without distorting the text's eucharistic application.

The beginnings of the process we have indicated

are already found in Mark 6:41a, where we see that although Jesus took the five loaves and the two fish, he broke only the bread. As he sometimes does precisely in eucharistic matters, Luke may witness to an older tradition when he implies that the fish originally formed part of the object of the verb "break" (9:16). By using the verb absolutely and grammatically without object, however, he demonstrated his uncanny ability to harmonize current practice with early tradition.

Taken together, the above observations indicate that the early Christian communities introduced subtle changes in the wording of the narrative in order to maintain and heighten the clarity of its eucharistic meaning. Each of these adaptive efforts was conducted in light of the current eucharistic practice and experience of the Christians who saw themselves in the event.

An additional indication of continuity in eucharistic interpretation may be found in the use of the substantive *klasmata* (Mk 6:43), which in the multiplication stories denotes the broken fragments left over from the meal. The term persisted in early Christian eucharistic language, but not without considerable transformation. In the Jewish-Christian community whose life is reflected in the *Didache* it was applied to the blessed bread about to be broken and shared.

We must not conclude that the early Christians viewed the multiplication of loaves as an early instance of the Eucharist which would constitute so important an element in the post-Easter life of the Christian communities. Transcending any such anachronism, however, they clearly saw that the miraculous feeding prefigured their Eucharist and could be fruitfully drawn upon to convey important aspects of its nature.

At the same time we must not minimize the fact

that the eucharistic interpretation placed the multiplication in a new light. In one sense, it is entirely appropriate to view the multiplication event as a pre-sacramental Eucharist in the historical life of Jesus. In another sense, the multiplication meal was already sacramental, with the historical Jesus acting as a human sign of God's presence and with the offering of food as a sign of Jesus' self-communication. Among those who accepted Jesus' gesture, the event effected an active participation in the very life and value-system of its author. Those who ate of the bread and fish in faith accepted a new relationship to Christ which gave them a share in the life of God.

For Christians who sought to establish a relationship between Christ's presence to them in the post-Easter Eucharist and the earlier historical presence of Jesus, the multiplication of loaves incident provided an important element of continuity. This continuity was such that the Eucharist could be traced back to the multiplication as to an important moment in its origins. Among the Gospel traditions the eucharistic multiplication of loaves antedates even the liturgical narratives of the Last Supper. Although the Eucharist was celebrated at a very early date in conscious continuity with Jesus' last historical meal with his disciples (1 Cor 11:23), the development of this tradition in the form of Gospel narrative appears to have come at a later date. As a result, it never acquired the universally recognized foundation or institution status already achieved by the multiplication story—so much so that in John's Gospel we must reach past the Last Supper to the account of the multiplication of loaves and the events which surrounded it for an understanding of the origins of the Eucharist. In this John was true to earliest tradition. By chronologically situating the multiplication near the feast of Passover (Jn 6:4), he was faithful to further traditions which related the Eucharist and its institution to this Jewish feast (cf. Mk 14:1).

The Life and Mission of the Church. The early Christians did not divorce their celebration of the Eucharist from other aspects of life in the Church. Accordingly, the account of Mark 6:34-44 shows itself extremely sensitive to the mission of the post-Easter Christian community.

First, we note that it is the disciples who initiated the discussions concerning the feeding of the crowd (v. 35). On simple grounds of historical verisimilitude, this action may reflect the original situation. To appreciate its persistence in the story through several decades of transmission, however, we must situate it in relation to two distinct tendencies in the tradition's development.

In order to accentuate the central role of Christ in the celebration of the Eucharist, one line of tradition tended to replace the disciples' initiative by that of Jesus. Thus it is that the leading role which Jesus exercised in taking, blessing and breaking bread for sharing spread to nearly all other parts of the account. This development, which is strongly reflected in Mark 8:1-9, corresponded to the growing christological concerns of the early Christians with regard to every aspect of Christian life.

At the same time, a second line of tradition tended to emphasize the relative but nonetheless essential function of Jesus' disciples in the eucharistic celebration. Although the Risen Lord himself continued to act in the Eucharist, it is through his faithful disciples that he lived and acted. Thus it is that in certain developments the role of the disciple rather than that of Jesus was accentuated. This phenomenon, which is well represented by Mark 6:34-44, corresponded to the Christian community's ecclesiological concern to continue Christ's mission in history.

In Mark 6:35-36, retention of the disciples' initiative may thus have been prompted by the narrator's interest in the role of the disciples who extended the historical work of Christ after his death. This seemingly insignificant detail thus corresponded both to the original event and to one of the major concerns of the post-Easter community.

The disciples had suggested that Jesus send the people away to find food for themselves. Jesus responded with a challenge: "You give them something to eat" (Mk 6:37). The full significance of Jesus' command becomes obvious when the passage is read from the point of view of his disciples' on-going mission to the crowds. In Jesus' response we sense the early Church's realization that it must not rely on the past work of Jesus but assume the responsibility he had shared with them. For Jesus' memorial to be truly effective, the disciples knew that they had to give human expression to his attitude, word and gesture. In this way they transcended the once-and-for-all which characterized the historical actions of Jesus and gave these actions new life in the over-and-over again of their liturgical celebration.

The early Christians' keen awareness that the risen Jesus continued to work through them is confirmed by their role in the remainder of the account. In each subsequent movement or stage in the event, Jesus involved the disciples: "How many loaves have you? . . . Go and see" (v. 38); "He told them to make the people sit down on the green grass in groups or parties" (v. 39);

"Then, taking the five loaves and the two fish, Jesus . . . broke the loaves, and gave them to the disciples to distribute" (v. 41); "They gathered up enough leftovers to fill twelve baskets" (v. 43).

The task of assessing the needs and resources of the hungry is assigned to the disciples. They it is who are commissioned to organize the crowd into communities. Theirs also is the task to distribute the nourishment which Christ himself continues to give.

The text places great emphasis on the leftovers. Gathered into twelve baskets, one for each of the twelve apostles who were placed at the head of the tribes of the New Israel, they indicate the Eucharist's relationship to the original multiplication event. In the years following Jesus' death and long after the miraculous feeding, the Christians continued to be nourished by Jesus' wondrous historical action through the service of his disciples.

Jesus' command that the disciples give the people something to eat is rich in pastoral implications. Challenged to take up the historical role of Christ, the disciples, and we along with them, are asked to assume his attitude of self-giving in our celebration of the Eucharist.

When in the name of the community the leader of the assembly speaks the words of Christ, "This is my body; this is my blood," he not only quotes the words of Christ but makes them his own. The leader's own person and life, and through him and that of the entire community, is placed on the line. It would be difficult to find a more eloquent expression of fraternal love and community solidarity.

Offering his life for his fellow participants in the

Eucharist, and indeed for all who are called to share in this meal, the priestly leader's personal sacrificial offering is an important part of the eucharistic sign or sacrament. For centuries, the Church's emphasis on the *ex opere operato* has tended to obscure this important aspect of the eucharistic meal. What was meant to correct a widespread tendency emptying the Eucharist of the Risen Christ has unintentionally led to the impoverishment of the eucharistic sign. The Second Vatican Council's *Constitution on the Sacred Liturgy* has reasserted the richness of eucharistic sacramentality by focusing our attention on the diverse signs of Christ's presence. Failure to heed its plea for fidelity to sound tradition could result in the reduction of Christ's words of eucharistic interpretation to sounding brass and tinkling cymbals.

Biblical Articulation

So far we have examined the original feeding event and the various insights of faith which related it to the Eucharist and to the life and mission of the Church. In so doing we have indicated many of the religious factors which influenced the event's formulation in primitive Church tradition. It now remains for us to see how the event was articulated in terms of biblical literature. Following their general practice, the early Christians reflected on Jesus' multiplication of loaves "according to the Scriptures." As we know from 1 Corinthians 15:3-5, for example, this practice long antedated the writing of the four Gospels. In Mark 6:34-44, it helped to shape the earliest strata of pre-literary tradition.

The most important biblical passage to influence our narrative is found in 2 Kings 4:42-44:

> A man came from Baal-shali-shah bringing the man of God twenty barley loaves made from the first fruits, and fresh grain in the ear. "Give it to the people to eat," Elisha said. But his servant objected, "How can I set this before a hundred men?" "Give it to the people to eat," Elisha insisted. "For thus says the Lord, 'They shall eat and there shall be some left over.'" And when they had eaten, there was some left over, as the Lord had said.

The relationship between this important passage in the Elisha cycle and the traditions preserved in Mark 6:34-44 is unmistakable. Not only do both narratives present an episode in which loaves are multiplied, but they do so in clearly parallel fashion. Like Elisha, Jesus orders that the people be given to eat. Like Elisha's servants, Jesus' disciples focus on the problem of feeding so many with so little food. In spite of this difficulty, however, the people do eat, and in both cases there is food left over. In verses 6, 9 and 13, John's narrative has even preserved the specification that the loaves were made of barley, a detail not taken up in other traditional developments.

A second passage to influence the multiplication narrative is Psalm 23 with its reference to the verdant or green pastures where God gives repose. In Mark 6:39 and in John 6:10, the people sit down on green grass. For his part John marvels that so large a crowd as five thousand would have found sufficient grass to find a place on the ground.

Reflection and meditation on the multiplication event in light of Psalm 23 may have been inspired by the Psalm's later emphasis on the celebration banquet which God sets out before his people (v. 5). Together with Elisha's multiplication of loaves, the Psalm thus focused attention on the generous quantity with which God nourished his people. Through this double prism the Christians thus came to see the Eucharist itself as an abundant nourishment.

In his redaction of the Jewish/Christian multiplication stories, Mark gave even further prominence to the imagery of Psalm 23. When Jesus looked upon the vast crowd, "he pitied them, for they were like sheep without a shepherd" (6:34). He then proceeded to fill the lack. Once again the Lord was their shepherd (Ps 23:1). Later, in the post-Easter life of the community, the disciples would continue his shepherding role. "You give them something to eat." The sheep must not be left without a shepherd.

Conclusion

The story of Jesus' miraculous feeding reaches out of the Church's origins and out of the pages of the New Testament to become *our* story. Christ's challenge is addressed to us: "You give them to eat." The ancient word pushes, chides, stirs and commands us to fill the expectant hand of the hungry, of an entire human race which will never be sated, for it is part of the human condition to yearn for that bread from heaven which alone will finally satisfy.

It takes courage and dedication to assume Christ's challenge, especially when so many open hands have closed into clenched fists, or simply fallen limp with all energy of expectation stilled. They had reached for Christ's nourishment; they were given an earthly *ersatz*, a gift empty of self and humanity, an uninvolved gesture which mimicked that of Christ but failed to imitate his self-offering.

But then we too are among the hungry, wondering where in ourselves we shall find nourishment for so many. It takes humility to accept our own hunger and our limited capacity to extend the hand of Christ. And then there is the cost! How much of ourselves can we afford to give? How far can we go without risk of personal dissolution? How far did Christ go? So long as our "this is my body" falls short of that of Christ, there will continue to be sheep without a shepherd.

Archaeological Witness to the Eucharist

Ernest Lussier, S.S.S.

In the art of the catacombs we have the first beginnings of Christian art before us. There is none earlier. Inscriptions, frescoes, and sarcophagal reliefs are the major types of art represented. The representations are simple yet graphic, and usually without backdrop of landscape.

The fish had already appeared in pagan art, but the Christians soon discovered that in the Greek language the five letters that spell fish form an acrostic, being the initial letters of the phrase, "Jesus Christ, Son of God, Savior."

Writing about 200 A.D. on Baptism, Tertullian states: "We little fishes, after the example of our fish, Jesus Christ, are born in water, and we cannot be saved if we depart from it."

Ambrose says that men are the fish caught by the fisherman, Peter, and that his hook does not kill but sanctifies. A very old inscription from the catacomb of Domitilla shows the cross as an anchor which has caught two little fish that represent the faithful. Augustine states that in the word fish "Christ is mystically understood because he is able to live, that is, to exist, without sin in the abyss of this mortality as in the depth of waters."

Thus the fish might stand symbolically for the name of Christ in an inscription reading, "Alexander in," after which a fish is shown completing the phrase "in Christ."

Or fishes might stand for the Christians themselves. A grave has the word fish followed by "of the living" which must mean, "Jesus Christ, the Son of God, the Savior of the living," adorned with two fishes which must represent the Christians who are the living.

The fish as a hieroglyph for Christ was also susceptible of varied application and remained a favorite theme of Christian iconography. St. Augustine's referring of the symbol to Christ's passion is interesting. Commenting on John 21:9, he remarks: *Piscis assus, Christus est passus* (The fish laid on the fire is the suffering Christ).

Christ as a fish was used in a special sense for Christ as food and thus for the Eucharist. The classical proof for this is the famous metrical inscription of Abercius.

In 1833, Dr. William Ramsay discovered in Asia Minor two large fragments of this sepulchral inscription. In 1892 this was given by the Sultan to Pope Leo XIII and now adorns the Lateran Museum at Rome. With the help of the epitaph of Alexander (a contemporary imitation) and a Greek biography of Abercius, it is possible to restore the entire text of the inscription.

Abercius was a bishop of Hieropolis, a small town in Phrygia. At the age of seventy-two he composed for his own tomb an epitaph in which he mentions his visit to Rome and to such faraway places as Syria and Mesopotamia. The date of the inscription is in the latter part of the second century.

The text is written in a mystical and symbolic

style, according to the discipline of the secret *(disciplina arcani)*, to conceal its Christian character from the uninitiated. This metaphorical phraseology was the occasion for a sharp controversy following the discovery of the monument. Several scholars have believed that Abercius was not a Christian but a devotee of the Phrygian goddess Cybele or a syncretist. A closer study of the text, however, has demonstrated beyond possible doubt that the content as well as the language of the piece is Christian in character.

Here is a translation of this queen of all ancient Christian inscriptions:

I, the citizen of an eminent city, erected this tomb in my lifetime, that I might have here in due time a resting-place for my body. Abercius by name, I am a disciple of the holy shepherd who feeds his sheep upon the hills and plains, whose eyes are large and all-seeing, who taught me the faithful writings, and sent me to Rome to see the royal city, and the queen robed in gold and wearing golden shoes. There I saw a people marked with the radiant seal. I also saw the plains of Syria and all the cities, even Nisibis, beyond the Euphrates. And everywhere I found fellow believers, having Paul as a companion, and everywhere faith led the way and set before me for food the fish from the spring, the pure fish of great size which the spotless virgin caught and ever puts before the friends to eat. She has also delicious wine and offers the mixed cup with the bread.

I, Abercius, dictated this to be written in my presence, in my seventy-second year. Let every fellow believer who understands this, pray for Abercius. Let no one lay another in my grave under penalty of 2,000 gold pieces to the Roman treasury and 1,000 to my beloved native city, Hieropolis.

The theological importance of this text is evident. This is the oldest stone monument mentioning the Eucharist. The language of Abercius is poetic and somewhat enigmatic but he expects fellow Christians to understand his mystic symbolism.

This inscription probably illustrates the *disciplina arcani*, the fact that from the second to the fifth century some care was exercised in certain quarters not to reveal to non-believers the Christian doctrine, especially relative to the sacraments of Baptism and of the Eucharist.

The holy shepherd of whom Abercius calls himself the disciple is Christ. The queen clad in gold must mean the Church in Rome, and the Christians are the people with the resplendent seal. The term seal for Baptism was well known in the second century.

Abercius presents himself as a world traveler, having journeyed as far west as Rome, and east even beyond the Euphrates. Everywhere he found fellow believers, and everywhere substantial uniformity in ritual. He is acquainted with the Sacred Scriptures, and his reference to St. Paul is probably an expression of his predilection for the Pauline writings.

Christ is the big fish from the spring according to the well-known acrostic. The Incarnation is described rather fantastically as Mary's catch of the fish, and strangely enough she is the one who offers this food to the Christians' friends. It could well be, however, that here the author's thought passes imperceptibly from Mary to the Church of which she is the prototype.

Christians everywhere partake of Christ in the observance of the Lord's Supper. The faithful receive bread as food and wine mixed with water, but faith tells them that it is really the great, pure fish, that is, Christ born of the Virgin Mary.

From the dogmatic viewpoint this inscription is of prime importance. Besides referring explicitly to the sacraments of Baptism and of the Eucharist, it supposes implicitly the divinity of Christ, the importance of the Roman Church, veneration for the virgin Mary, and the communion of saints.

Another beautiful poem of the fourth century refers to Christ as the fish. It is known as the inscription of Pectorius and was found in an ancient Christian cemetery not far from Autun in southern France. The first five verses form the Greek acrostic ichthys.

Divine race of the heavenly fish, draw with a pure heart, ye mortals, from the immortal fountain of divine water. Refresh your soul, my friend, with the perennial waters of wealth-giving wisdom. Take the honeysweet food of the Savior of the saints; eat with joy and desire, holding the fish in your hands. Lord and Savior, I pray, satiate us with the fish. I beseech you, light of the dead, may my mother rest in peace. Aschandius, my father, so dear to my heart, and my beloved mother and my brothers, in the peace of the fish, be mindful of Pectorius.

The references to Baptism and the Eucharist are again quite clear. Baptism appears as "the immortal fountain of divine waters" and the "perennial waters of wealth-giving wisdom." The Eucharist is described as "the honeysweet food of the Savior of the saints."

Christ in the first line is the heavenly fish, and again in the sixth and seventh stichs. The use of the term Savior three times is also meaningful. Finally, the ancient Christian ritual of receiving communion into the hands explains the words "holding the fish in your hands."

St. Cyril of Jerusalem, among others, describes this ancient rite. The communicant received the body of Christ in the palm of his right hand, saying: "Amen." He was warned to be very careful not to lose any particle of the sacred bread. He then partook of the consecrated cup, bending low and saying again in the way of worship and reverence: "Amen."

One of the most ancient catacombal paintings symbolizing the Eucharist is found in the crypt of Lucina and dates back to the middle of the second century. It appears on the wall of a chamber and consists of two symmetrical representations of a fish to the right and to the left of a central piece.

A basket full of round small loaves rests on each fish, or at least is so close in front just above the tail as to seem to rest on the fish. Inside the basket is a glass of wine which the artist depicted as showing through the mesh of the side. The configuration of a cup is clear enough and a red blur unmistakable as representing wine. If, as seems quite probable, the fish represents Christ, the intimate relation of the eucharistic elements with the body of the Savior would be graphically illustrated. In any case, there can be no doubt about the fundamental eucharistic signification of the whole, and of its Johannine overtones.

Because there are two fishes facing each other, it has been thought that they represent the faithful who live in Christ and by Christ, and that the water under the fishes is symbolic of Christian baptism. This little problem could perhaps be clarified if the subject matter of the missing central panel were known.

Banquet scenes are frequently portrayed in the catacombs with fish and bread, and sometimes wine, as the components of the feast. It is not always certain, however, whether these scenes depict the meals that were taken in honor of the dead, or represent the Lord's Supper itself, or the heavenly banquet.

In the cemetery of Priscilla there is a fresco called the *Fractio Panis* (Breaking of the Bread), a name given it by Wilpert, its discoverer. It is found in the Capella Graeca and is the oldest known representation of the Eucharist, dating back before the middle of the second century.

Seven persons are gathered in a half-circle (sigma) around a slightly rounded table on which are placed a plate with two fishes and another with five small round loaves of bread. Seven bread baskets are ranged on either side of the table, four to the left (as one looks) and three to the right. The third guest from the right is a veiled woman, her presence inculcating probably the universal character of the gathering.

The person on the extreme left has his hands outstretched and somehow his feet are clearly seen above the table. This is probably due to the artist's failure in perspective, in his effort to make this character more conspicuous. In any case, a large cup with two handles is before him, and he is apparently breaking one of the loaves, while the second, fourth, sixth and seventh (left to right) banqueters are attentive to his action. The third and fifth (the woman) are looking the other way, perhaps simply for artistic variety.

This fresco may be the oldest representation of the eucharistic rite. It is not absolutely sure, however, that the bread is really being broken, since that portion of the painting is badly damaged.

Another portrayal of the Eucharist and the sacrifice of the Mass is found in the cemetery of St. Callistus in the Sacrament Chapel A3, and is dated at the beginning of the third century.

A man dressed as a sacred person and a philosopher (with pallium and tunica exomis) stretches out his hands in benediction over a small three-footed table on which bread and fish are laid. The pallium is the Latin name for the Greek himation—a long shawl sometimes hard to distinguish from the toga, but much less voluminous. The exomis is sleeveless and short. Sacred persons were commonly depicted in a white pallium, and the exomis was characteristic of Greek philosophers.

To the right stands a woman (orant) with her hands uplifted in prayer, symbolizing, no doubt, the Church.

The Eucharist most probably is portrayed here. It is not clear, however, whether the man is Christ or the priest in the act of consecrating. Yet, it seems certain that the fish and bread are symbols of the Eucharist. It is also well known that in Christian antiquity the altar had normally the shape of a table; in fact, the altar was simply called a table (mensa). Even today, mensa is the term used to designate the flat surface at the top of the altar.

A similar table with a fish and two loaves is found on the vault of a ceiling in Callistus. The loaves are marked with a cross. To the side of the table are seven baskets of bread. The date again is the end of the second or the beginning of the third century.

There are several examples of mystical meals in

the chambers of the sacraments at St. Callistus. The figures are always seven, the baskets usually seven (but also eight or ten). Seven is simply the number of perfection according to ancient biblical symbolism.

What dominates in most of the banquet scenes is the eucharistic signification. The idea of funeral agape, if present, remains in the background. At times, however, the stress seems rather on the heavenly banquet of the blessed, leaving implicit the eucharistic symbolism.

The banquet as a symbol for heaven is a common theme in the New Testament. This idea of the celestial banquet appears in later catacombal art in the third and fourth centuries. For example, in a fourth-century fresco in the catacomb of Peter and Marcellinus, four guests recline upon a semi-circular sofa around a sigma table. Peace and love are personified as servants and everything points to the peace, abundance and refreshment to be expected in the life to come. One of the guests cries, "Peace, give me warm wine"; another, "Love, mix me wine." Both are asking for the calida, a drink of wine mixed with warm water. Wine was commonly drunk warm, and always mixed with water because of the high alcoholic content necessary to keep the beverage for any length of time in bottles of skin or clay.

The sight of a shepherd carrying a sheep on his shoulders is familiar in the Middle East today, and representations of this subject are found not only in Greco-Roman times, as, for example, in Hermes Criophorus (Ram-Bearer), the protector of flocks who carries a ram on his shoulders, but also much more anciently. In Assyria and Syria, reliefs have been found from the eighth and tenth centuries B.C. which portray a man bearing a gazelle on his shoulders, while the statue from

Mari of a man carrying a kid in his arms is as early as the third millennium B.C. These older figures represent worshipers bringing animals for sacrifice, but at least by the time of the ram-bearing Hermes of Greece, and perhaps much earlier, the idea of the good shepherd was current.

In Christian art, the type was conceived anew and filled with Christian meaning. It appears much more frequently in the catacombs than any other symbol. Styger has counted 120 paintings and 180 plastic representations of this figure. The good shepherd is now Christ himself who carries the lost sheep back to the fold. God in the Old Testament had also been represented as a shepherd (Is 40:11; Ez 34:12). The image of the good shepherd is thus a biblical illustration of God's providence and of the redemption wrought by Christ.

The particular appropriateness of such a symbol in Christian sepulchral art is plain enough. The shepherd in the Old Testament Psalm 22 leads his sheep through darkest gloom, a thought which is clearly most apt for Christian burial.

It is interesting to note that the good shepherd is the only theme in Christian art which was often presented as a statue. The early Church frowned upon carving, which was considered as easily leading to idolatry. But this shepherd idea was so plainly a symbol that it was not very likely to be abused.

The famous statuette of the good shepherd, usually dated in the third century, which is now in the Lateran Museum in Rome, may have originally stood in a cemeterial crypt. It shows the shepherd as a beardless youth, still in his teens, whose curly hair falls upon his shoulders. He wears a tucked-up tunic and high stockings, and has a basket slung on a strap. He carries the lost sheep gently on his shoulders.

The good shepherd is usually surrounded by his flock in the garden of his paradise. In the catacombs the presence of flowers and trees serves to indicate the celestial paradise. A Christian would easily see here a symbol of the peace of the redeemed, of those who live in Christ even after death.

The juxtaposition of the orant and the good shepherd is found as early as the painting in the Lucina crypt, where in alternating corners of a ceiling fresco are found two shepherds and two orants. This combination recurs frequently thereafter in Christian art, and its significance is unmistakable. The Christian prayer for deliverance in time of need and death is answered by the good shepherd who carries the soul safely home to its fatherland in paradise.

Later the good shepherd was depicted in the performance of the activities of his idyllic profession. In a third-century fresco from Peter and Marcellinus, Jesus holds a shepherd's pipe in his right hand. In a fresco from Callistus, the good shepherd carries a pail (mulcta) of milk symbolizing the Eucharist. In a crypt of Lucina, the pail of milk is placed on a small altar guarded by two sheep.

The eucharistic symbolism of the milk is corroborated by the celestial visions of the martyr Perpetua (A.D. 202). The good shepherd appeared to the saint in a garden, surrounded by his flock. He was milking and gave her some of the curds, while those standing by said "Amen." In this vision of paradise she receives the proffered food as she received the Eucharist on earth according to the same rite, in the hands, while all those present say "Amen."

Ewes' and goats' milk was a staple food in biblical times, as it is still today in the Near East. Consequently, the Christian writers of the third and fourth centuries saw in milk the elements of flesh and blood. After the fourth century, the figure of the good shepherd in Christian art seems to have been rapidly displaced by the apocalyptic Lamb of St. John's Revelation.

Representations of a woman with arms uplifted in prayer, like that of the shepherd with a lamb on his shoulders, were also familiar in Hellenistic art. This figure recurs with great frequency in the Christian art of the catacombs but is invested with special significance. It is well known as the orant and reflects the Hellenistic tendency to personify abstract ideas, a distinctive Christian figure, a personification of prayer for salvation and a symbol of Christian devotion. The early Christian writers explain the attitude of the orant as an imitation of Christ on the cross. The position was the biblical posture for prayer, especially of praise and thanksgiving.

Since the orants are occasionally shown in the garden of paradise and have the name of the departed written nearby, it is clear that they were also regarded as symbolic representations of the deceased. Some interpreters have suggested that the soul of the deceased is thus portrayed as praying for the loved ones still on earth. It seems more probable that the holy soul is represented as giving thanks for its salvation, or even as still praying for the ultimate redemption which includes the resurrection of the body.

In the Christian frescoes of the catacombs there is little about Jesus' life story as such; only those features which served the special interests of the Christian community at that time were portrayed. Thus there is considerable interest in the two sacraments of Baptism and the Eucharist.

Early Christian art avoided representing any of the episodes of the passion in a manner which would reveal their stark reality. No painting in the catacombs of the first centuries does so. Before the fifth century the cross was rarely represented in catacombal art. It was usually symbolized by an anchor, or a dolphin over a trident.

How Our Fathers in the Faith Prayed

The Sacrifice of Praise in Early Liturgies

John Barry Ryan

How shall we pray at the eucharistic celebration? Ask this question in a parish church of the Roman Rite in the Americas, Africa, Europe and Asia, and you will receive a very simple answer: use the Roman canon or one of the three 1968 eucharistic prayers or, on occasion, one of the more recent prayers for reconciliation or for Masses with children. This kind of answer misses the point. It is like the one students give when asked, "What do you want to get out of this religion course?" "An A, what else?"

In the early Christian centuries, when local churches had great autonomy in their prayers, the above question had real importance. This was long before the rise of the major rites. Rather it was a time when, more often than not, eucharistic prayers were freely composed within the limits of a well-known outline.[1]

What did one say in eucharistic prayers in the eastern Mediterranean area around 100 A.D., at Rome around 215, in the Nile Delta toward 350, and in

Syrian Edessa in the fourth century? At a time of possible heresy or schism, when single words caused long, sharp debates, how did one pray in the midst of the assembly? How did the presiding person publicly praise God in the presence of the bread to be eaten and the cup to be shared?

That great care was taken with such prayers is seen from the manuscript context in which they have survived the centuries. Some scholars think that a eucharistic prayer is found in the *Didache* or *Teaching of the Apostles*. Another is surely found in the *Apostolic Tradition*. This is especially noteworthy, for Hippolytus, its author, in opposition to Pope Calixtus, wishes expressly to link his instruction and prayers to what was handed on at the foundation of his church, even though his eucharistic prayer is a model rather than a fixed text.

The prayer collection of Bishop Serapion (d. 362), disciple of the famous Anthony of the desert and friend of the great Athanasius, appears as a normative handbook. Bishop of Thmuis in lower Egypt, Serapion is an authoritative figure, influenced by the expression of the champions of the true faith, yet not without a certain ambiguity.[2]

The *Prayer of the Apostles* is that of the putative founders of the church in Edessa, Syria. Sometimes called the *Anaphora* (prayer of offering) *of Saints Addai and Mari*, it has particularly created discussion among scholars in an area where disagreement is the rule rather than the exception.[3]

All these names are meant to be impressive because the prayers were destined for local churches. When a particular region was evangelized, the people who became the Christian community or church there were given the liturgy of the founders. In the course of time, this liturgy was often expanded, shortened, paraphrased or improved (for example, made more biblical!) for one reason or another.[4] Nonetheless these prayers enjoyed great authority, for it was especially at the Eucharist that Christians overflowed with praise and thanksgiving for what Jesus revealed to them about the past, taught about the present, and told about the future.[5] In a hostile world, subject to periodic outbreaks of persecution and accusations that they were atheists, outlaws in the worst sense of the word, Christians frequently had to pay a high price to worship. In good times, however, they could often become dull about the joys of their faith and even succumb to competing faiths.

What, then, do these early prayers tell us about these Christians of the early centuries? How did their prayers reflect some of their own particular emphases, and how did they relate their sacrifice of praise to their lives?

Didache

Chapters IX and X of the *Didache*, despite the impatience of some recent scholars, cannot be said to present eucharistic prayers properly so called, but they contain nonetheless Jewish-Christian thanksgiving prayers for the cup of wine (as in Lk 22:17) and then for the bread.[6]

The cup thanksgiving is for the holy vine of David, the bread thanksgiving for life and knowledge, all of which are revealed through Jesus. It was to David that the promise was made; his vine issues in Jesus, the fulfillment of the promise. From Jesus comes eternal life as well as knowledge of the wonderful deeds of God in our behalf. Thus, through Jesus we have access to a knowledge otherwise unknown. Without him, the Father's plan and its fulfillment would have remained veiled. The mystery is that God had so ordained and brought it about through Jesus (Eph 1:4-10).

The cup prayer and the bread prayer are said in the course of a regular meal. At the end of the meal, additional thanksgiving prayers, in the manner of the Jews, are extended over a whole range of themes, all of which appear to be at the same time Christian versions of Jewish thanksgiving prayers as well as elaborations of the Lord's Prayer.

These prayers show the closeness of Jesus to people. Where there are doubt, confusion, suspicion and competing doctrines, Jesus brings true and sure knowledge. The Jewish Christians of the *Didache* are now more certain than ever that God created the world so that he might be praised. He gave men good things, food and drink, but also, as their meal shows, a nourishment that leads to eternal life. These Christians are not despisers of life, but possessors already of gifts beyond their imagination.

Nor do they fear the future, for they look forward to being assembled from the ends of the earth into the kingdom prepared for them. The whole context of these prayers, containing allusions to the paradise imagery of Genesis as well as the banquet prepared by Wisdom (Prov 9:1-6), presents a grandiose picture of Jewish eschatology. These Christians pray so well that we can only admire this great gift of Judaism to Christianity: a high style of prayer based on the Bible.

Apostolic Tradition

Well over a hundred years after the *Didache*, Hippolytus, a priest and later an anti-Pope, who in the Maximinian persecution ended up slaving in the salt mines of Sardinia and dying a martyr's death with Pope Pontian, presents a stunning model of a eucharistic prayer. This is the prayer whose adoption was urged ten years ago when the Roman Rite was ready to enlarge its euchology. It was, of course, adapted rather than adopted, becoming Prayer II, the familiar short one.

The least that can be safely said of Hippolytus' prayer is that it represents a prayer composed at Rome. But of all the prayers of that time anywhere, it has had the most celebrated history and influence. Already it contains the essential structure and content of later eucharistic prayers.

Hippolytus gives thanks to God through Jesus Christ. Unlike later Oriental anaphoras that will have a developed theological praise of God followed by a christological one, this prayer announces its theme and carries it through: "We give thanks to thee, O God, through thy beloved Child, Jesus Christ. . . ." The remainder of the prayer, what we would call the preface, illustrates this. Referring to the Son as God's "inseparable Word," Hippolytus' every phrase dwells on the connection between the Father and the Son: *your* Child, *you* sent him, Savior, Redeemer and Messenger of *your* will, through him *you* created all things.[7] It is clear that the Father is praised through the Son and it is because of this concrete dynamism that it is unthinkable for Hippolytus to have a preface of divine contemplation.

Nor does he have a Sanctus, and hence, also, no

myriads of angels that will inhabit other anaphoras and fire the imaginations of their authors, in some cases taking up a large part of the prayer. Hippolytus is down to earth!

Just as the word "inseparable" pointed up the relationship of Father and Son, now the word "willingly" signals a new emphasis.[8] Jesus was no plaything, no passive instrument in the hands of Fate. So the link with the Father falls to the background:

> When he gave himself up willingly to suffer
>   to destroy death,
> to break the fetters of the devil,
> to trample hell under his feet,
> to spread his light abroad over the just,
> to establish the rule.
> and manifest his resurrection,
> he took bread. . . .

Such a prayer portrays a powerful Christ, very much active in overcoming evil. His death is not something endured; rather it accomplishes victory on a cosmic scale. We are reminded of the forceful Byzantine images of Christ. This is true whether or not grammatically it is through Christ's suffering or through the taking of bread that all these things are accomplished by Jesus.

The prayer thus becomes even more christological as it moves toward the words of the Lord at the Last Supper. The institution narrative is clearly part of a whole and it does not have the solemnity it will have in the Roman canon or later eucharistic prayers. It is not a consecratory piece, that is, the words of the Lord are not yet considered words of consecration. Rather the emphasis is on the words: "When you do this, do it in memory of me." The narrative gives warrant to what the Church is doing, namely, offering the bread and the cup and giving thanks in memory of the death and resurrection of Jesus Christ.

This is connected to the invocation that follows:

And we ask you to send your Holy Spirit on the oblation of the holy Church. In drawing them together, give to all those who participate in our holy mysteries, to be filled with the Holy Spirit for the confirmation of their faith in the truth.

The Holy Spirit through the Eucharist is called on to make one those who receive it. He is also the one who strengthens the Christians' faith in the truth. This passage has the priestly prayer of Jesus as its background, especially "Sanctify them in truth. Thy word is truth" (Jn 17:17) and "That all may be one" (Jn 17:21). It took the Roman Rite almost 1,500 years before it recovered such explicit invocations of the Spirit. Even then, it has been suggested, by choosing to have an epiclesis before the institution narrative and one after for the fruits of communion, the authors of the 1968 prayers did not return sufficiently to the earliest tradition.

Euchology

Serapion's preface is carefully constructed to develop by way of paradox. After the opening statement proclaiming the justice of praising God, the uncreated is called inscrutable, indescribable and incomprehensible. Such is the situation that exists between the un-

created God and the created nature. We would be at an
impasse were God not known to Jesus, the only begotten, who makes known his Father, who in turn reveals
the glory of the Son to the holy people.

In his opening words, Hippolytus referred to Jesus
Christ as God's beloved *pais* (child, servant, son)
whereas Serapion, over a hundred years later, refers to
Jesus as the uncreated Father's *monogenes* (only-begotten Son).[9] This word shows the distance traveled from a
servant christology to one that emphasizes the nature of
the Son. In either case, of course, those who subordi-
nated the Son to the Father, even in his divinity, could
interpret the passages as they wanted. The change in
wording, however, is symptomatic of a new situation. It
is more than a question of combating those who would
deny Christ's real flesh and blood or even his real will;
there were those who would make him a lesser god.
Thus, the prayer insists on the Son as only-begotten
against the Arians. It is not so much a dogmatic theological language, as we might think, but the popular
religious language of the time. Its repetition appears
frankly didactic.

The prayer goes on to praise God as the invisible
Father who gives immortality, who is the source of all
life, light, grace and truth. This Father loves men and
women, he loves the poor, and he reconciles everything
to himself. Through the coming of his beloved Son, he
draws everything to himself.

Before such a splendid God, lover of humankind,
the thanksgiving turns into petition. "Make us living
men and women! Give us the spirit of light so that we
may know thee, the true one, and him whom thou hast
sent, Jesus Christ."

The prayer concludes by asking for the Holy Spirit
who enables men and women to tell forth indescribable

mysteries. We have come full circle. At the outset, the Father is indescribable, in the middle the Son has revealed him, and at the end the Holy Spirit is the enabler who gives men the power to expound the holy mysteries. And with the words, "May he celebrate thee with hymns through us," the prayer moves toward a ringing Sanctus that leaves no doubt as to the power and majesty of God.

It is quite a different prayer from that of Hippolytus. It is more magnificent and more rhetorical about the greatest mysteries. It is no longer christological. Rather it celebrates the deeds of the Father.

Serapion's Christians prayed at the Eucharist in other ways that are different from those of Hippolytus' faithful. He gives more solemnity to the institution narrative by introducing an invocation of the Holy Spirit, thereby cutting the section off from a flowing prayer of praiseful thanksgiving. In the middle of the institution narrative, which starts off with the solemn introduction of Paul, "For the Lord Jesus, the night when he was betrayed" (1 Cor 11:23), we are surprised to find a prayer from the *Didache*:

> For just as this bread,
> once scattered upon the hills,
> has been joined together to become but one,
> so, too, deign to reunite thy holy Church
> from every people, from every land,
> from every town, village and house,
> and make her one single Church, living and catholic.

No longer is the request clearly eschatological as in the *Didache*. Here the plea is pressing: the unity of the

Church has been racked by schism, even within house-holds.

Is this why Serapion also invokes the Word on the bread and the cup? Such an invocation would show the sanctifying action of the Logos, and hence, it has been argued, his divinity.[10] Furthermore, the effects are precise: the transformation of the gifts (into the "body of the Word" and "the blood of the Truth") and the fruits which flow from them for the participants (a life-giving remedy that heals every infirmity and strengthens for all progress). These Egyptian Christians are not the idealized community of the Book of Acts 2:42-47. They are painfully aware of their sins and their need to move forward. This is surely one reason why abbreviated intercessions are introduced into the eucharistic prayer itself.

Finally there is a more elaborate address to God than is found in the other prayers. In place of the simple "Father" of the *Didache* and the "O God" of the *Apostolic Tradition*, we have "O eternal God," "eternal Father of the only-begotten," "invisible Father," "Lord of Powers," "God of Truth." Something has happened since the early years. The invocations reflect new ways of talking about God occasioned by theological controversies, the vicissitudes of everyday life, and an incantatory style of praying.

Anaphora of the Apostles

This prayer may be as early as that of Hippolytus or later than Serapion's. While it has some similarities with the prayer of Hippolytus, the differences are more striking. For one thing, the people of this prayer would

not think of saying with Hippolytus, "We give you
thanks for having judged us worthy to stand before you
and serve you," even if this refers to an episcopal ordination. Rather they prefer, "You have exalted our
low estate and restored our fall . . . and made the
weakness of our frail nature triumph by the abundant
mercies of your grace."

God is everything; man in comparison is nothing.
These people are marked by the fall but even more by
their marvelous redemption. They are simply over-
whelmed by their salvation. Yet, there does appear to
be a certain preoccupation with self, even if it is to
express unworthiness, "We . . . weak, frail and misera-
ble servants . . . stand before you at this time." Nevertheless, there is something very right about this insistence on "us." Humankind is intimately related to God
in creation and redemption.

The prayer proceeds by way of repetition and a
piling up of synonyms and adjectives that reflects a
spirit different from the other prayers. Not only is the
same thing said twice, it is sometimes said three times
or five times. When stripped of later interpolations that
comparative textual analysis reveals, it is found to be a
very ancient prayer indeed. It is unique in being a
thoroughly Semitic prayer, strongly influenced by the
form and style of Jewish prayers. For example, it is
addressed to the Son, who is called the Name:

> Worthy of praise from every mouth and of confes-
> sion from every tongue and of worship and exalta-
> tion from every creature is the adorable and
> glorious Name who created the world by his grace
> and its inhabiters by his mercifulness, and saved
> mankind by his compassion and gave great grace
> to us mortals.

This glorification of the Name probably comes from the *Qaddish* recited at the synagogue service. The Christians used it to show their allegiance to Jesus considered under the title of the Lord who triumphed over death. In fact, this may be the primitive starting point of the eucharistic prayer that later would be enlarged to include praise for the whole history of salvation.[11]

Finally, what has drawn the particular attention of scholars to this prayer is the absence of an institution narrative in the manuscript tradition.[12] This in itself is no proof that the words of institution were not recited. It would be speculation on our part to suggest reasons for this. Scholars are divided on this problem as they are divided over many things in all of these prayers.

What cannot be doubted, though, is that the early Christians reflect different emphases and exhibit different styles of praying. Semitic and Hellenistic influences abound. In orthodox and less orthodox expressions, theological development is seen. From the long perspective of the centuries there is always a tendency to lump the millions of Christians scattered over space and time. No matter, at the heart of their eucharistic assembly these early Christians testified in public praise that God through his Son, Jesus Christ, had saved them and given them a future to hope in. Their publicly acknowledging this around the eucharistic gifts was their sacrifice of praise.

Thus, in the beginning there was diversity, then in the major rites there came uniformity, and now with the presence of nine eucharistic prayers and eighty-five prefaces in the Roman Rite, we have returned not so much to diversity but to a diversity within a uniformity. It may well be that the next step is a genuine diversity.

The eucharistic prayers of the early Christians represent an attempt to praise God from within the context of their own culture, tradition, and theological emphases. If it becomes the experience of pastors and parishioners that the revised Roman Rite does not take root in our people, then it may mean that the time for a legitimate diversity will have arrived. If that day comes, we can look forward to eucharistic prayers being composed in our own language, expressing our own concerns, yet still rooted in a tradition that has taught us how to pray. When the silent Roman canon was proclaimed in English aloud, the eucharistic prayer retained its central place, but now a new demand was made upon it. No longer was it the awe-inspiring prayer of mysterious rites. It was the prayer of public thanksgiving and praise of particular people who are the local church. The consequences of this change still remain to be drawn.

NOTES

1. This is not the same as some present-day spontaneous prayer. Improvisation in the early Church meant that traditional patterns with key phrases were followed. When these improvised prayers became suspect, there was a move toward fixed formulas which were already in use in the rites of the sees of major cities.

2. For some there is much that is ambiguous in the prayer; for others, like Dom Botte, the final redactor of the *Euchology* is an Arian (or at least an Arian sympathizer) and surely someone who is opposed to the Holy Spirit's being given too great a place. In any case, the anaphora would not be an original production of Serapion because it antedates even him. Cf. Bernard Botte, "L'Eucologe de Sérapion est-il authentique?" *Oriens Christianus* 48 (1964), 50-56.

3. Most recently in William Macomber, "The Oldest Known Text of the Anaphora of the Apostles Addai and Mari," *Orientalia Christiana Periodica* 32 (1966), 335-371,

and "The Maronite and Chaldean Versions of the Anaphora of the Apostles," *Orientalia Christiana Periodica* 37 (1971), 58-66. See also Emmanuel J. Cutrone, "The Anaphora of the Apostles: Implications of the Mar Esa'ya Text," *Theological Studies* 34 (1973), 624-642.

4. This is true of liturgical texts in general. Cf. Hieronimus Engberding, *Das Eucharistische Hochgebet der Basileiosliturgie*, Münster, 1931, lxxvi, and Anton Baumstark, *Comparative Liturgy*, rev. Bernard Botte, tr. F. L. Cross, Westminster, Md., 1958, 23. A privileged locus for this is the institution narrative. See F. Hamm, *Die liturgischen Einsetzungsberichte im Sinne vergleichender Liturgieforschung untersucht* (LQF 23), Münster, 1928.

5. Or as it is put in the *Letter of Barnabas* 5, 3: "We ought to give great thanks to the Lord that he has given us knowledge of the past and wisdom for the present, and that we are not without understanding for the future," in *The Apostolic Fathers*, tr. Kirsopp Lake, Vol. I, London, 1965, 355.

6. Bouyer has no doubts that they are eucharistic prayers because, he says, these *Didache* prayers parallel Jewish texts and follow the traditional meal blessings. They therefore apply to a sacred meal of a Christian community still close to Judaism. The meal of this community could only be its Eucharist. Cf. Louis Bouyer, *Eucharist*, tr. Charles Underhill Quinn, Indiana, 1968, 117. This opinion is supported by Klaus Gamber, *Sacrificium Laudis: Zur Geschichte des fruhchristlichen Eucharistiegebets*, Regensberg, 1973, 35. But Jungmann in his latest book says: "Some authors still believe that in the prayers in chapters nine and ten of the *Didache* may be traced not only table grace for the feast day meal of the Jewish Christians but eucharistic prayers as well." The place of the word "still" in this citation needs to be verified in the German original. Cf. Joseph Jungmann, *The Mass: An Historical, Theological and Pastoral Survey*, ed. Mary Ellen Evans, tr. Julian Fernandes, Collegeville, Minn., 1975, 22. Thomas Talley, however, in a very nuanced position is between Bouyer and Jungmann. See "From *Beraka* to *Eucharistia*: A Reopening Question," *Worship* 50 (1976), 129.

7. Since the word "inseparable" has theological implications as well, it was not used in the adaptation of Hippolytus'

prayer in the revised Roman Rite. See Pierre Jounel, "La Composition des nouvelles prières eucharistiques," *La Maison-Dieu*, No. 94 (1968), 47.

8. For "willingly" see Jn 18:4 and Is 53:7.

9. *Monogenes* has an early history in the Christian communities as Jn 1:18 and 3:16 reveal. See T. E. Pollard, *Johannine Christology and the Early Church*, Cambridge, 1970.

10. Lucien Deiss, *Early Sources of the Liturgy*, tr. Benet Weatherhead, second edition, Collegeville, Minn., 1975, 117, argues by analogy with the practice of the Church Fathers who used the sanctifying work of the Holy Spirit as a starting point for proving his divinity. But Dom Botte, *op. cit.*, 55, says that the redactor, not Serapion, substituted the Logos for the Holy Spirit deliberately in order to downplay the role of the Spirit. Both authors used Dom Capelle to support their argument. Deiss simply follows Capelle's conclusion that the use of the Logos is an innovation by Serapion. Botte, while accepting Capelle's demonstration that the practice of using the Logos in the epiclesis was not a current one in Egypt around 350 A.D., rejects Capelle's hypothesis of Serapion's originality in favor of his own concerning an Arian redactor who wishes to downplay the Spirit even more than he does the Logos. See Bernard Capelle, "L'Anaphore de Sérapion: Essai d'Exégèse, *Le Muséon* 59 (1946), 425-443.

11. Cf. Robert Ledogar, *Acknowledgment: Praise-Verbs in the Early Greek Anaphora*, Rome, 1968, 161-163.

12. For a summary of this in a larger context, see Talley, *op. cit.*, 130-135.

The Presence of Christ in the Eucharist

Reflections on Christ's Eucharistic Presence as Participant and as Nourishment

Eugene A. LaVerdiere, S.S.S.

At the end of the short preface to his Gospel, Luke indicates his intention to bring readers to "true understanding in matters concerning which they have already been informed" (1:4). I find no better expression for my own purpose in the following pages.

Belief in the Lord's eucharistic presence has been a constant element of Christian faith from the earliest days of the Church. Each new generation, however, is called upon to reflect upon this faith and personally appropriate it. Otherwise, faith affirmations all too easily become divorced from life experience. Our challenge then is clear. If eucharistic faith is to remain operative in the life of Christians, it must be clearly related to our actual faith experience.

It is with this challenge in mind that I have explored the New Testament for a deeper understanding of Christ's presence in the Eucharist. Limiting my reflections to Christ's presence in the eucharistic celebration, I concentrated yet further on his presence in the

participants and in the nourishment, prescinding from
other aspects of eucharistic presence such as in the
word. In so doing, I focused on the close relationship
between nourishment and participant both in the historical life of Jesus and in his metahistorical or risen life.

Eucharistic Origins

The origins of an institution such as the Eucharist
may be situated at a number of historical moments.
Prior to examining its roots in the historical life of
Jesus and in the post-Easter experience of the early
Christian community, we must carefully fix our point
of departure. Otherwise we risk general confusion or
loss of continuity, either of which would nullify our efforts.

Since the Eucharist as we know it is essentially
characterized by the presence of the Risen Lord, we
might with good reason begin its history with the assemblies of the earliest post-Easter communities. Accepting this option, our inquiry would focus on the historical relationship between faith in the Risen Lord and
eucharistic experience.

Although we cannot define the precise moment in
history when Christians first recognized the Risen Lord
in the context of meal fellowship, the New Testament
data require that this have taken place at an extremely
early date. Indeed it may be that the birth of Easter
faith coincided with that of eucharistic faith. According
to both Luke and John, most if not all of the appearances of the Risen Lord occurred in the context of early
Christian meals. In Acts, this same relationship is even

more clearly affirmed in the Petrine discourse to the household of Cornelius (10:40-41). However, even if Christ did manifest himself to Peter and the disciples prior to and outside of those early meal experiences, it remains true that meals taken after Jesus' death became truly eucharistic only when the Christians encountered the Risen Lord in their breaking of bread.

The origins of the Eucharist can also be traced beyond the table of the Risen Lord to the historical life of Jesus. Many of the eucharistic texts narrated or otherwise presented in the New Testament indicate that the early Christians quite universally related the Eucharist to Jesus' mortal historical life. Several of these texts attach the Eucharist to the meal which Jesus shared with his disciples on the night before he died. Others reach even further to the time when Jesus multiplied the loaves and fishes for a vast crowd which had gathered to hear him or even to the "multiplication" of the wine which had become insufficient at Cana. The blessing prayers of the *Didache* relate the Eucharist still more generally to the totality of Jesus' historical work with his disciples.

New Testament texts bearing on Jesus' historical life carefully situate the Eucharist with regard to the broader range of Jesus' activities such as healing and teaching. They also present Jesus in a twofold relationship to his disciples. The latter both partook of meals with Jesus and shared his role of leadership in nourishing others. The roots of the Eucharist in the life of Jesus were thus seen to be extremely extensive, reaching into the whole of his life among men. Given these considerations, we should not be amazed at the New Testament's emphasis on the many meals which

Jesus took with his disciples or at its sensitive articulation of their theological and even eucharistic significance.

Consequently, although a history of the Eucharist
may justifiably begin with the risen life of Jesus, it is
equally possible to start with meals which the historical
Jesus shared with his disciples, and such will be our
point of departure. Admittedly, the pre-resurrection
narratives reflect the post-Easter faith and preoccupa-
tions of the Christian communities from which they
stem. This very fact, however, indicates an awareness of
continuity between the pre-Easter and the post-Easter
Christian meals.

Meals in the Historical Life of Jesus

In the course of his earthly mission, Jesus shared
many meals with diverse groups of followers, actual
and potential. The Gospel texts speak of meals taken
with the poor, the rich, the uneducated, the learned, the
little people, and the powerful. These same texts dwell
lovingly on meals enjoyed in the company of close
friends and with the small band of disciples. There were
simple meals, banquets, festive meals and traditional
religious meals. Different in many respects, all of these
meals were strongly marked by Jesus' presence and personal communication.

The meals of the historical Jesus were not unlike
those of the future Christian communities. In all their
variety, the post-Easter meals of Jesus' followers were
chiefly characterized by Jesus' presence. Careful not to
minimize the significance of Jesus' new risen state, we
may nevertheless affirm that the critical difference be-

tween these meals and the pre-Easter meals lay primarily in the mode of Jesus' presence.

The above observations are not without theological implications. Focusing on the difference between pre-Easter and post-Easter meals, we have come to view Jesus' presence at the former almost exclusively in the role of participant and Christ's presence at the latter primarily if not exclusively as nourishment. A stress on similarity and continuity, however, forces us to inquire into the meaning of nourishment at Jesus' historical meals and into Christ's participatory role at the table of the risen Lord. In both cases, our questions remain the same. How was Jesus Christ present in the meal? How did these meals constitute a communion in his person? How were they sacrificial?

Presence as Participant. During his earthly years, Jesus was present at meals primarily and most obviously as a participant. Indeed this aspect of his presence is so obvious that its significance may altogether escape us, whereas it provides the best point of departure for all further reflection on Jesus' meal presence.

As a participant, Jesus shared in meals as one person among others. He thus held a position at table and related to others within a complex matrix of roles and attitudes. Essentially, these attitudes may be summarized in the term presence. Jesus was present *qua* person to others *qua* persons. Such presence involved attentiveness to others, respect, receptivity, an attitude of active openness not to be confused with passivity, and extension of self or reaching out to others.

Sharing in food together was thus the concrete physical expression of a much broader and deeper sharing attitude. Obviously, meals were not the only locus or situation in which Jesus shared, but they undoubtedly did represent a high point and a privileged moment of sharing. Such sharing extended beyond ideas, projects and spoken attitudes to include the very person. By sharing in the same meal or life-source, the participants expressed their desire to share of themselves and be united in one life. In this context, we can appreciate the long biblical tradition of expressing covenant life relationships by joining in a common meal. The early practice of designating the Eucharist as a (new) covenant in Christ's blood (i.e., life) was thus continuous with fundamental human experience of meals and not a mere relationship of theological reason with an ancient biblical expression.

The attitude of the participant was strongly sacrificial in intention, inasmuch as all personal sharing expressed both the willingness to give of oneself and actual self-giving. In the case of Jesus, self-gift held no reservations. As an open-ended gift, Jesus placed himself on the line for others even if this should mean laying down his very life that others might live. Solidarity implies self-less risk.

The early Christians showed themselves keenly aware of the sacrifical implications of meal sharing when they repeatedly related the liturgical words of interpretation to the night before Jesus died. The cross proclaimed the full dimensions of the upper room. Good Friday was already implied in Holy Thursday. Paradoxically, disinterested self-giving is rich in returns. In Jesus' case, total gift of self brought fullness of life in the resurrection. The ultimate implications of Holy Thursday were thus revealed only on Easter Sunday.

Jesus' presence at meals must be further specified in terms of his relationship to other participants. Jesus did not limit his meal fellowship to those who already could be classed as his disciples. There were those like Zacchaeus to whom Jesus extended salvation by his personal presence at the family table. By receiving Jesus into his home and subsequently communing in his person, Zacchaeus played host to salvation (Lk 19:1-10).

At table with his disciples, Jesus was present as rabbi or master. Sensitive to this relationship, Jesus nourished his followers in their very discipleship. As a result, the latter developed to the point where their position vis-à-vis Jesus was transformed into that of friends and associates in Gospel ministry. The disciples thus grew in the same attitudes which characterized Jesus' presence at meals. Like Jesus, they too would one day face their Good Friday. The upper rooms of the early Christian communities were likewise rich in the hope of Easter.

In all of these meals it is obvious that Jesus did not participate absolutely as an equal but as one who presided over the meal. While Jesus' fundamental attitude may be shared by all who participate in the Eucharist, certain aspects of that attitude are relevant especially for those who are called to a role of leadership in the eucharistic assembly. Like Jesus, such Christians bear a responsibility not only to share of themselves but to elicit like attitudes of sharing and presence in all who gather at the Lord's table.

Presence as Nourishment. Having reflected on Jesus' presence as participant, we are now in a position to inquire into the significance of the nourishment itself. It is not sufficient to state that partaking of the same dish, loaf or cup expressed unity of life. More specifically, we must ask whether the food elements

themselves signified the presence of Jesus and effected
his self-communication.

Divorced from Jesus' gesture and attitude as a participant, it would remain difficult to see how the
nourishment could have meant anything more than
food for human sustenance. By abstracting the bread
and other elements from the total meal context, however, we would hardly do justice to the reality of a meal
with Jesus. Our attention must focus not on the food as
a reality in itself but as something offered by Jesus to
those who shared with him in a meal.

Our subject then is not precisely the food, but food
offered by Jesus, or, even better, Jesus' offering of
food. Indeed, this is what we read in the narrative in-
troductions to the liturgical texts included in the Last
Supper accounts as well as in many other New Testament texts: Jesus took bread, offered a blessing,
broke it and gave it to those present. Such texts lose
most of their force when we separate quoted words of
Jesus, such as "This is my body," from the action
which they mean to interpret.

In order better to situate the nourishment, it may
be helpful to visualize it in the very hand of Jesus
reaching out to the other participants as well as in the
hands extended to receive it from Jesus. In actual fact,
not all nourishment was so transmitted, but the correlative gesture does enable us to appreciate what was implied in Jesus' action of sharing food.

In the social context of a meal, bread and other
food were clearly not intended merely to feed the belly
of the participants. Such a reduction of meals with
Jesus to an act of animal feeding would stand in clear
contradiction with every interpretation given these
meals by the New Testament. Rather, the food which
Jesus offered signified the entire manner in which he

reached out to others and extended his person to fill the personal void of those who hungered for life and embarked on a new way of salvation as his disciples. In other words the nourishment was a concrete *sign* of Jesus' personal salvific presence to those with whom he joined in the meal. Offered and received, it also *effected* the mutual presence and personal union of life which it signified. As an efficacious sign or sacrament, it consummated the other dimensions of personal communication which characterized meals with Jesus.

An example drawn from a contemporary life situation illustrates the strong relationship between nourishment offered and the person offering it. When a child has been punished by his parents for wrong-doing, he may not immediately recognize the love which prompted the action of his father and mother. Consequently, when food such as a piece of bread or cake is consciously offered him by his parents, he finds it difficult in himself to accept it. Unconsciously, he identifies acceptance with a reconciliation for which he may not be prepared. To accept the bread would be to accept the parent. The bread is thus seen as the concrete sign of the parent who now reaches out to him. When he does accept the bread, he accepts the parent, and reconciliation is effected.

From the experientially founded relationship of the food elements to the person of Jesus, who offered himself by offering the food, we can now understand how nourishment is a sign efficaciously communicating the life and person of Jesus to others. The sacramental values of the Eucharist are thus firmly rooted in the meals shared by Jesus during his historical life-span. We submit that the same dynamic relationship between Jesus' presence as nourishment and his presence as participant underlies the post-Easter Church's appreciation of eucharistic bread and wine as the body and blood of Christ.

At the Table of the Risen Lord

The post-Easter meals of the early Christian community, and indeed our own eucharistic meals, pose a problem quite opposite that of the earlier meals with the historical Jesus. Whereas in the latter we needed to expand our awareness of the significance of nourishment in relation to Jesus' presence as a participant, in the former we need to reflect especially on the Lord's presence as a participant.

Presence as Participant. Much has been written in recent years on the New Testament's presentation of the resurrection of Jesus. It is not our purpose to go over this research or even to indicate its major conclusions. We mean rather to focus on one single aspect of the appearance narratives, namely, that Jesus is present as one who eats with his disciples. That this was not merely a by-product of the narrative form may be seen from Peter's discourse to the household of Cornelius:

> They killed him, finally, hanging him on a tree, only to have God raise him up on the third day and grant that he be seen, not by all, but only by such witnesses as had been chosen beforehand by God— *by us who ate and drank with him after he rose from the dead* (Acts 10:40-41; cf. also 1:4).

A witness to Jesus' resurrection was one who shared in the eucharistic meal with Jesus after God raised him from the dead.

As Jesus of Nazareth, Jesus had participated in many meals with his disciples. Since his presence as a participant was the primary and the most obvious form of his earlier self-communication, it was only normal that the Christians would continue to think of him in this way. As Risen Lord, he thus continued to share meal fellowship with his disciples.

Even the accounts of the Last Supper emphasize this same mode of presence. In Luke's Gospel, Jesus looks forward to the day when he will once again join in a meal with his disciples (22:16, 18). It is also in this context that we can best understand an expression like the table of the Lord (Lk 22:30; 1 Cor 10:21). The early Christian breaking of bread was a sharing in the Lord's table because the Lord himself was seen to preside over the meal.

At this point it becomes necessary to introduce an important historical distinction. We must not assume that early Christian awareness of Christ's presence was uniformly articulated from the first experience of his risen life to the ninth and tenth decades of the first century when the Gospel accounts of Matthew, Luke and John were cast in definitive form. In doing so we would hardly do justice to the very strong eschatological note which pervades the earliest eucharistic texts.

At first, the Christians who gathered for the Lord's Supper did so in memory of Jesus' action and personal sharing at meals taken during his historical years and especially in memory of the eucharistic event which preceded the consummation of his earthly work. They were thus extremely aware of Jesus *absence* at least according to the normal mode of being which characterizes this-worldly human life. Further, they looked forward to Christ's return on the Day of the Lord when he would once again partake of a meal with them. Fullness of life in the new age was thus expressed in the classical prophetic imagery of a messianic banquet. Eschatological hope for the future, no less than memory of the past, reveals a strong sense of Christ's absence in their meals at least for a time. In this early context, absence must be taken in reference to his earlier presence as a visible and numerically distinct participant.

It was only natural that during this earliest period of post-Easter eucharistic history the Christians would focus on the nourishment as an enduring sign of Christ's presence. The nourishment, however, was seen as one which *had been given* by Christ and which now continued to sustain them. Hence the emphasis granted the left-over fragments in the multiplication narratives. The bread which Jesus had so abundantly provided was sufficient to nourish the community until Christ's second and definitive coming.

Later, with the attenuation of apocalyptic expectations, the early Christians were bound to come to a new awareness of Christ's presence in the Eucharist. The unfolding of history acquired definite Christian value. The Christians themselves became living signs of sacraments of Christ's presence in history. The messianic banquet had already begun and its clearest manifestation lay in the meal celebrations of the early Christians.

With the development of post-apocalyptic attitudes, it once again became possible to view Jesus present as a participant at the meal. The Risen Lord shared in the eucharistic meal in the person of his followers, and he presided over the meal-assembly in the leader of the Christian community. Obviously, this mode of participation was quite different from that of the historical Jesus, but it was nevertheless a genuine presence of Christ as participant in the meal.

Because of the difference in Jesus' mode of presence and especially in view of the fact that the Christian manifestations of Christ's presence remained imperfect, the Christians continued to celebrate the Eucharist in memory of Jesus' ideal self-communication and in anticipation of his glorious return at an undetermined future moment. During the intermediate time, however, they could still join with Jesus at table. It was for them to perfect the sacrament of Christ's presence by their own attitude as participants.

Presence as Nourishment. With new awareness of Christ's presence as participant, it became possible once again to view the eucharistic nourishment as one which was actually being given by Christ rather than as one which had been given. In the new post-Easter context, however, the attitude of presence and sharing among the Christian participants took on new and critical importance. It was for them to give concrete expression to Jesus' one-time historical action. Any impoverishment in their attitude affected the liveliness of the community's faith in Christ's presence as nourishment. Experientially, such faith depended in large measure on the felt relationship between the nourishment and the mutual presence of the participants.

Since Christ was no longer visibly present as a numerically distinct participant, the nourishment derived its sign value from the Christian hand and gesture which offered it to the other participants. To appreciate what was now required of the Christians who gathered for the meal we have but to reread our reflections on Jesus' presence as a participant during his historical years.

The sacrifice of Christ had become the community's sacrifice, and communion in Christ's life was realized in the life of the community. Paraphrasing Paul's famous line, we can say that for each Christian to be present was Christ. The bread which the Christians offered and shared became weighty with their gift of self, and in so doing it gave sacramental expression to Jesus' own gift. As we have seen, Jesus himself had educated his disciples in this attitude during the very meals which they had earlier enjoyed with him.

On the basis of the foregoing discussion, it becomes obvious that any contemporary malaise concerning the real presence of Christ in the Eucharist may stem from our divorcing Christ's presence as nourishment from his presence as participant. For its part, such a divorce might well spring from a sad diminution of eucharistic attitudes on the part of those who celebrate the Eucharist. Far too frequently, we merely repeat the words and action of Christ with no realization that our own lives are deeply implicated in the eucharistic action. What was meant to be word and action has become mere sound and motor coordination.

Failing to give properly human expression to Christ's eucharistic attitude, we strip the eucharistic signs of all but the bare minimum and seriously test the faith of those who might still be searching for Christ and inquiring whether the Eucharist might not be the locus of Christ's presence to them. Then there are all those who affirm belief in the real presence, but only because others have told them that it is so. No longer do they believe on the basis of their own experience. What was meant to be a source and shaper of Christian identity has become a mere source of Christian identification.

Our challenge is clear: a role of leadership in the Eucharist is for that person alone who assumes Christ's eucharistic attitude of self-giving. Awareness of the weakness of our present sacramental value must become a point of departure for growth as each day we speak Christ's words of eucharistic interpretation: "This is my body; this is my blood." So may it be. It is not sufficient for Christ's presence to be real in itself. He must be really present for us.

Christ's Presence
in the Liturgy

Edward J. Kilmartin, S.J.

Catholic theologians have always taken for granted Christ's abiding presence to the world in virtue of his glorification. They distinguish this cosmic presence from his personal presence in the believer (Eph 3:17) and to mankind through the exercise of faith of all believers and through the service of the ordained ministry in word and sacrament. However in the Western Church, especially since the Reformation, most of the emphasis has been placed on Christ's presence under the eucharistic species.

Only in recent years have Catholic theologians begun again to rethink the ancient belief concerning the variety of real presences of Christ within the whole scope of Christian life. They have been led to attempt, in various ways, to relate the different modes of Christ's personal presences to one another. Nevertheless in all the various proposals at least one common element is found: the concern to preserve intact the uniqueness of Christ's presence in the liturgy and to affirm the Lord's Supper as the highest ranked personal presence of Christ within the liturgical celebrations of the Church.

In the last twenty-five years the Magisterium of the Roman Catholic Church has likewise called attention to the different modes of personal presence of Christ in the life of the Church while stressing the uniqueness of his liturgical presence. The initiative was taken by Pius XII in the encyclical letter *Mystici Corporis* (September 29, 1943). Here he recalls the personal activity of Christ in the whole life of the Church with special mention of the celebrations of the sacraments.[1] This latter topic was developed by him in the encyclical letter *Mediator Dei* (November 20, 1947). His summary of the modes of presence of Christ in liturgical celebrations[2] served as the basis for Vatican II's presentation in the *Constitution on the Sacred Liturgy*, no. 7. At the close of Vatican II Paul VI also referred to the subject of Christ's presence in the Church with specific reference to the liturgy. In the encyclical letter *Mysterium Fidei* (September 3, 1965) he alludes to the *Constitution on the Sacred Liturgy*, no. 7. However it is noteworthy that he follows more closely the development of this theme as found in the original schema of the *Constitution on the Sacred Liturgy*.[3]

A comparison of the last four mentioned documents yields the following:

Mediator Dei: Christ is present (1) in the eucharistic sacrifice in the person of his minister; (2) "especially" under the eucharistic species; (3) in the sacraments "by his power"; (4) in the prayer of the Church (Mt 18:20).

Original Schema of Constitution on the Liturgy: Christ is present (1) in the gathered community (Mt 18:20); (2) in the word of Scripture; (3) in the prayer of the Church; (4) in the sacraments and eucharistic sacrifice.

Constitution on the Sacred Liturgy: Christ is present (1) in the eucharistic sacrifice in the person of his minister; (2) "especially" under the eucharistic species; (3) in the sacraments "by his power"; (4) in the reading of Scripture; (5) in the prayer of the Church (Mt 18:20).

Mysterium Fidei: Christ is present (1) in the prayer of the Church (Mt 18:20); (2) in works of mercy; (3) in preaching the word of God; (4) in the exercise of ecclesial authority; (5) "in a more sublime way" in the eucharistic sacrifice through the ministry of the priest; (6) in the sacraments "by his power"; (7) "especially" under the eucharistic species.

For our purposes we may note the following similarities and differences between these presentations. All these documents teach that the Church's activity in word and sacrament is a means of salvation because of the abiding active presence of Christ in the Church. They all emphasize the special degree of Christ's presence in the liturgy and single out the eucharistic celebration as the most intensive form of his presence. *Mediator Dei* and the *Constitution on the Sacred Liturgy* begin the enumeration with the Eucharist while *Mysterium Fidei* and the original schema of the *Constitution on the Sacred Liturgy* first make mention of Christ's presence in the faithful community. Thus these latter two documents reflect the traditional theological conviction that Christ's presence in the community of faith is a condition for his other modes of personal presence in the liturgy. Still none of these presentations attempts the task of showing how the different modes of Christ's presence in the liturgical celebrations are related to one another.

It is the responsibility of systematic theology (1) to enumerate the various modes of Christ's real presence in the Church; (2) to show how they are related to one another; (3) to explain why the presence of Christ in the liturgy is the highest ranked representation of Christ's real presence in the Church; (4) to show why the eucharistic presence is the most intensive form of Christ's real presence within the liturgical celebrations of the Church. In the following pages the outline of such a presentation will be presented.

We can begin with a consideration of how Christ's personal presence was concretely realized in the world after his death. It is clear that the resurrection of Jesus Christ makes this possible. However the glorification of Jesus does not take place in the time and space of history. It is an act of God by which Jesus Christ participates in the fulfillment of history! Hence the Risen Lord must make himself accessible within history. Herein lies the theological significance of the appearances of the Risen Lord to the disciples. In allowing himself to be seen (1 Cor 15:5-8), Christ simultaneously bestows the gift of faith in his continuing presence "for them" in the "chosen witnesses" (Acts 1:8).

Concerning the chosen witnesses we can say that Christ made himself present to them through his appearances as the conscious content of their act of faith. But he also made himself present *in them*: as sharing source, with the Spirit, of their act of faith. This leads us to conclude that the presence of Christ in the believer, as sharing source of faith in his abiding presence, is basic to all other modes of personal presence of Christ in the Church.

But in what sense is the presence of Christ *in the believer*, as sharing source of faith in his abiding presence, basic to all other modes of presence of Christ in the Church? Is it the source from which all the other modes of presence unfold? Is the personal presence of

Christ in the Church realized only by the exercise of the faith of which Christ is the sharing source? We can agree that when a believer witnesses to his faith by preaching and loving service, this is a means by which Christ becomes personally present to the one who hears the word or sees the service done in faith since he is the source of the exercise of this faith.

But is there another way by which Christ becomes personally present to mankind and which operates independently of the exercise of faith of believers? Are there institutions established by Christ to which he binds his presence and which operate independently of the exercise of the faith of the Church? Are there institutions which have a function analogous to the Easter appearances? Certainly the Easter appearances were not dependent on the exercise of faith of believers. They were the inner-worldly way by which Christ made himself accessible to the disciples while creating faith in his abiding presence. Are there institutions which operate in this way?

Two alternatives lie before us: 1. Christ effects faith (a) by the Easter appearances independently of the exercise of faith of believers; (b) by the exercise of faith of the "chosen witnesses" and their followers; (c) by institutions independently of the exercise of faith of believers. 2. Christ effects faith in his abiding presence by the Easter appearances, and all other modes of his personal presence are dependent on the exercise of faith of which Christ is the living source.

These alternatives offer two approaches to the relationship between faith and institution. The first approach understands that faith is mediated by the exercise of the faith of the "chosen witnesses" and their followers *and also* by institutions which operate independently of the exercise of faith: by the institution of apostolic office, the institutional word of God and the sacraments instituted by Christ. In the latter mode of mediation of faith the Risen Lord is understood to render himself personally present through the faith which he creates concerning his presence in office, word and sacrament. Here office, word and sacrament are conceived as fulfilling the function of the resurrection appearances which were not dependent on the exercise of the faith of believers.

The second approach affirms that the personal presence of Christ is never inwardly independent of the exercise of faith except in the case of the resurrection appearances (prescinding from the problem of "private revelations"). This alternative seems correct.[4]

The "chosen witnesses" are so on the basis of the faith which Christ effects. They are equipped for their mission by the gift of faith. The special role of Peter, for example, is based on a special charism of faith according to Luke 22:31-32. The content of office of the "chosen witnesses" is their obedient exercise of their faith in Christ's abiding presence which they represent by words and actions (Acts 3:4-16).

These witnesses constitute the Church. Bound together by the same faith, they form the New People of God. But they are likewise sent in full power on the grounds of their faith. Hence their faith vis-à-vis those who come to faith through their witness appears at the same time as office. However in the communities which succeed this original community, office does not have the character of "eye-witness," i.e., derived directly from the appearances of Christ and his commission. In these latter communities, office derives from the faith of the Church and its authority from the fidelity to the faith of the Church which is mediated by all believers. Accordingly the presence of Christ in the exercise of office appears as a special mode of exercise of the fundamental presence of Christ in the faith of the Church.

What can be said of office in a general way can also be said of the presence of Christ in the preaching of the word and the celebration of the sacraments. The word of God spoken in the Church is the word of Christ *and* the word of the Church. However we do not have two different words. Rather we have to do with a word of the Church of which Christ is the living source. The word of God is not so dissociated from the exercise of faith that the personal presence of Christ through the word preached is mediated independently of the exercise of the faith of believers. No "inspired word of God" exists in the Church which takes over the function of the Easter appearances. Christ does not make himself present in the Church through a word which is only his word and not the word of the Church.

The Apostles clearly understand that they are servants of the word of God. However, their service consists in the obedience of faith to which they are enabled by the Risen Lord. The Apostles (Paul especially makes this clear), are convinced that they preach the word of God if they witness to their faith. For them the word of God exists in the world in the form of a believing answer. In their confession which proclaims their faith, Christ is present because he, as the living source of this obedient exercise of faith, effects this exercise of faith. The abiding presence of Christ in the world is only accessible through the word which witnesses to the faith of which Christ is the source. Faith comes from hearing the word (of faith) of a believer.

Since the word of faith of the Church is an essential aspect of the sacramental celebration, the *forma sacramenti*, what is said of the word of God can be said of the sacraments. The sacramental word which expresses the meaning of the sacramental symbolic action is an ecclesial word of faith. Therefore the faith of the Church is constitutive of the personal presence of Christ in the sacramental celebration. It is the way by which the sacramental action, instituted by Christ, is realized.

Briefly, in the sacramental action the faith of the Church expresses itself and represents itself: the faith of which Christ is the living source. Since the faith represents itself it can represent nothing other than Christ and his redemptive act. Hence it renders Christ personally present as the source to which it is indebted, as well as the formative norm of its expression.

But if we grant that all the modes of presence of Christ in the Church are realized through the exercise of faith, how should we explain the special mode of Christ's presence in the liturgical exercise of the faith of the Church? The *Constitution on the Sacred Liturgy* makes a qualitative distinction between the modes of presence of Christ in the exercise of faith of the individual Christian and the gathered community. Christ is said to be present "especially in its liturgical celebrations" (no. 7). On what grounds can these degrees of presence of Christ be explained? What aspect of the liturgical event makes it the highest ranked representation of Christ's personal presence?

To answer this question we should look to the peculiar nature of the liturgical event: a *celebration* of the faith. But what is characteristic of a celebration? First of all the words and actions are not directed to the opportunities and demands of ordinary life. They are employed to call attention to the permanent values which are present in ordinary life. They are detached from their ordinary meaning and purpose in such a way that they become constants. One thinks of the various rites and words traditionally associated with a wedding feast. In the case of the liturgy, for example, the word "father" signifies the ultimate and permanent source of all concrete parenthood; the water bath means the purification and renewal of the whole person.

Moreover in a celebration the participants can become representatives of a larger reality. For example, a whole family is represented at a family feast even when some of the members are absent. In the case of the liturgy, the whole Church is represented by the gathered local community first and foremost because it is a celebration of the faith of the Church.

Only through the celebrating community is Christ fully represented as the one who already unites the people of God and gives a share in the graces of the Kingdom. The mode of faith celebration makes the full reality of the abiding presence of Christ present as no other mode: it represents by itself *(ex opere operato)* Christ's personal presence, and represents it as already imparting a share in the final blessings in the yet unfulfilled world. Other exercises of the faith do this according to the measure of their actual influence on the conditions of this world *(ex opere operantis)*. Hence liturgical celebrations are, as Vatican II says, "the summit to which the activity of the Church is directed and the source from which its power flows."[5]

Our reflections have brought us to the final question which concerns the various modes of Christ's presence in the liturgy. We have explained through the concept of celebration why the liturgy is a special mode of the personal presence of Christ. Now we will have to explain the differences and relationship between the various modes of Christ (not of course the fact of his presence) from the peculiar function of word, symbolic gesture and gift in the realm of human communication.

We may begin by observing that Christ presents himself in the liturgical event in the mode of celebrating the faith. In the liturgy the community affirms itself and represents itself. It expresses its faith and so represents Christ who is source of the faith. Christ's presence remains mediated by the exercise of the faith of the Church.

Now in the liturgy the various modes of expression admit of degrees, and so the specific mode of presence of Christ in the different elements of the liturgical events should be explained by these modes of expression. As in ordinary human relations the participants of the liturgy are present to each other (and so to Christ) differently in words, symbolic actions and gifts. But it should be noted that the various forms of expression are complementary ways of personal self-representation, all of which complete one another. Hence if one mode of presence is emphasized to the detriment of the other—even if it is the most intensive—the full representation is obscured.

Words and symbolic actions are prominent among the different forms of self-representation. The word can only be received by hearing (the spoken word), symbolic actions by seeing. While seeing allows us to develop certain attitudes toward a person, it is not sufficient to make the other fully accessible to us as a person. For this the word is indispensable. Hence the word is more important than appearances for the representation of the person. Yet both pertain to full presence. The word makes the person present; in the appearances the person is or remains present. All this holds true for a festive celebration. The festive word reveals the grounds for the celebration but it does not, by itself alone, represent fully the fellowship and appear as festive by symbolic action.

In the liturgical celebrations of the Church the community fully represents itself to itself by word and symbolic action. In so doing it fully represents Christ's abiding presence in its midst. The common word represents Christ as Lord of the Church; the dialogue represents Christ as the one who unites believers among themselves. By symbolic gestures Christ is represented as the one who is present sharing the blessings of salvation. Word and symbolic action are not in competition. Together they represent the full reality of the abiding Christ. And this representation reaches its climax in the eucharistic presence through the action of the Spirit who transforms the bread and wine into the body and blood of Christ and thereby enables the most intensive form of personal communion with the Incarnate Lord.

This gift of the Bread of Life affords the most privileged place of growth in the life of faith, of union with the Father through the Incarnate Son. Hence it is with right that the *Constitution on the Sacred Liturgy* states that Christ is present in the liturgical celebrations of the Church "especially under the eucharistic species." This presence and communion, however, are only profitable for those who have first heard this word of the Church and believe, through Jesus Christ, that it is a word of Christ: "As the living Father has sent me, and I live because of the Father, so he who eats me will live because of me" (Jn 6:57).

NOTES

1. *Acta Apostolicae Sedis* 35 (1943), nos. 50, 53.

2. *Encyclical Letter of Pope Pius XII on the Sacred Liturgy* (Boston, Mass.: St. Paul Editions, 1947), p. 11, no. 20.

3. *Encyclical Letter of Pope Paul VI: "Mysterium Fidei"* (Boston, Mass.: St. Paul Editions, 1965), pp. 16-17; *Acta synodalia sacrosancti concilii oecumenici Vaticani secundi* I/1 (Vatican City, 1970), p. 265.

4. The argument for this alternative has been developed at length by B. Langemeyer, "Die Weisen der Gegenwart Christi im liturgischen Geschehen," in O. Semmelroth (ed.), *Martyria, Leiturgia, Diakonia* (Mainz, 1968) 286-307. Most of what follows is dependent on this article.

5. *Constitution on the Sacred Liturgy*, no. 10.

Faith and the Eucharist

Joseph M. Powers, S.J.

In order to appreciate fully the role of the eucharistic community and its worship in the growth of the Christian in faith, hope and love, it is important to call attention to a significant change in focus for the theology of the sacraments. From the time that Peter Lombard (d. 1160) applied the notion of causality to the sacraments, sacramental theology could be characterized as a "theology of confection." The questions and concerns of sacramental theology centered on the conditions which are required for the sacraments to "produce their effect"—sanctifying grace and the other graces proper to each of the sacramental events. Aside from some marginal considerations of the requirements on the part of the "subject" or "recipient" of the sacrament, the major consideration was devoted to the powers of the minister of the sacrament, his ordination, unity with the Church, and so on. Drawing on a newly developed treatise on the Church which was centered on papal, episcopal and priestly power, sacramental theology emerged as a similar "power theology" largely concerned with who has the power to do what to whom.

This is the spirit in which St. Thomas Aquinas approaches his explanation of the sacraments in his *Commentary on the Sentences*, and it is the emphasis adopted by the Council of Trent in its defense of the theological tradition of the Church in its canon on transubstantiation. Accordingly this is the emphasis which found its way into the theological textbooks of the seventeenth, eighteenth and nineteenth centuries. It is the emphasis which has been found in much of the understanding, preaching and piety of approximately the last seven centuries. As it is applied to the understanding of the Eucharist, this theological style focuses on the power of the priest to "confect" the "real presence" of the Risen Jesus in the Eucharist, with all the consequences this has for the understanding of the Eucharist as sacrament and sacrifice, for the power of the Eucharist to confer the graces and virtues proper to it as sacrament. This is also the emphasis which characterizes Pope Paul VI's encyclical *Mysterium Fidei* in which he stresses the importance of the Eucharist for the fostering of the "sense of being Church" *(sensus ecclesialis)*.

But all this emphasis on the effective power of the sacraments has a particular and important context. That context is set by the classical formulation of St. Augustine when he describes the sacraments as "sign of a sacred reality" *(signum rei sacrae)* (*De Civitate Dei*, X, 5). Peter Lombard certainly develops his understanding of sacraments in this context, because the power and efficacy which he presents is the power and efficacy of a sign *(signum efficax gratiae)*. It is in this context that Thomas Aquinas develops his theology of the sacraments in the *Summa Theologica* (q. 60ff.) and the *De Veritate* (q. 26) where he insists that the sacraments "cause" grace by "signifying" grace *(significando causant)*. And it is to this context that Vatican II's *Constitution on the Sacred Liturgy* turns. For, rather than repeating Trent's declaration that Christ is "really present" by the "transubstantiation" which takes place by the power of the words of consecration spoken by the priest, Vatican II stresses the fact that it is the presence of Christ *throughout the entire liturgical action* which gives the liturgy its value as an act of worship and sanctification.

For in the constant worship which Christ offers to his Father, he always associates the Church with himself. Thus, he is always present to the Church, especially in its liturgical action. He is present in the minister of the Eucharist, and especially present in the eucharistic elements, in the word proclaimed, and in the singing and praying congregation (n. 7). However, this unfailing presence of Christ to the Church must be matched by the full presence of the faithful to Christ. And that full presence to Christ and through him to the Father, although it should rise to expression in the knowing, active and fruitful participation of the faithful in the Eucharist (n. 10), must also be the pattern of the whole of Christian life, a life of constant conversion and repentance shown in the works of love, piety and apostolate (n. 9). In this statement the Council consciously moves away from the kind of sacramental optimism which would place all the emphasis on the proper performance of the liturgical sacramental act, away from a narrow concern with requisites for validity and liceity of celebration to a strong emphasis on active participation in the Eucharist and, more importantly, to a presentation of the Eucharist as the self-conscious self-articulation of the whole quality of life in the community.

We could characterize this shift of emphasis as a shift from a theology of "confection" in which the principal concern is the proper performance of the ritual, to a theology of "celebration" in which the emphasis is rather on the quality of participation in the Eucharist. This quality of participation includes not only the elements of conscious and active participation in the liturgical action in prayer, song and communion, but extends beyond the liturgical community to encompass the whole life of the worshiping community. And in this, the Council proposes far more than a reformation of liturgy. It calls for far more, for a broad and deep renewal in the faith-life of the Christian community. This is a far more profound pastoral challenge because it calls on us to examine, judge and renew the whole pattern of faith-in-action which is Christian living. For the "celebration" in question is far more than a matter of flowers, balloons and banners. It is the honest assessment, acceptance and confession of who we actually are as believing Christians here and now, an acceptance and confession which looks to a deepening of the bonds of faith, hope and love which make of us a Christian community—an acceptance, too, of the weakness, division and pride which seek to tear those bonds asunder.

St. Paul urges the Christians of Corinth to this kind of "celebration" in 1 Corinthians 11. What is lacking in that community is precisely the vision which a full life of faith gives to the believer. The divisions, the selfishness and greed, the lack of concern for the brothers and sisters of the community indicate to Paul that the wealthy members of the community do not "discern the body" and thus "eat and drink judgment" (1 Cor 11:29). The judgment is not simply something which awaits these people in the future. It is in their midst in the weakness, neglect and even the death of those who make up the body. It is this judgment which is eaten when one fails to "discern the body." Vatican II calls for this same kind of "celebration," a celebration which includes "examining ourselves, and so eating the bread and drinking the cup" (1 Cor 11:28). For what rises to expression in the Eucharist as Jesus associates us with himself in his worship of the Father is the vision and experience of faith, a vision and experience which is not simply limited to the actual celebration of the Eucharist, but which extends beyond the liturgy to the whole fabric of our lives of faith as Christians. "Mysterium fidei!" ("The mystery of faith!") the deacon cried in the ancient liturgy, and the community responded with praise to God for the life, death and resurrection of Jesus, a mystery lived out daily in the vision and experience of lives of faith. In that experience of the profession of faith in the celebration of the Eucharist, their whole lives of faith rose to humble and jubilant expression and were deepened in their communal confession.

Vision and *experience*: perhaps these two words can best express what we mean by the substance of faith in our lives. Our faith is a perspective on life in the world from which we see ourselves and the world in a certain way, through which we experience ourselves and our world in a certain way, and because of which we find the courage to invest the limited but real power of our own freedom in ourselves and our world the way we do. The central vision of Christian faith springs from the confession that in raising Jesus from the dead and pouring out his Spirit to gather the Christian community together, God has definitively revealed who he is: the God and Father of the Lord Jesus, who raised him from the dead and who will give life to our mortal bodies through the Spirit which dwells in us (Rom 8:11). This mystery of faith is the core of the vision and the experience of the Christian in the world, and it is at the core of the Christian community as it gathers to celebrate the Eucharist. It is this mystery that we cele- brate with joy and hope in prayer, song and commu- nion as well as in the confession of our own sinfulness knowing that God is faithful and just (1 Jn 1:9).

This faith-vision and the experience it gives rise to are not something that we can arrive at through our own individual effort. Christian tradition has insisted on this, especially in the context of the Pelagian con- troversies in which the teaching of the Church laid great emphasis on the fact that faith is always grace, always gift. It is not reason or logic which brings us to Christian faith, but grace and gift. In this context, the importance of the living, worshiping Christian commu- nity becomes apparent. There may be those among us who find themselves thrown to the ground like Paul and experience dramatic, miraculous conversion. But for virtually everyone the bearer of the gift and grace of faith is the living worshiping community which says: "That which we have seen and heard we proclaim also to you, so that you may have fellowship with us; and our fellowship is with the Father and his Son Jesus Christ" (1 Jn 1:3). And the "proclamation" in question is far more than a preached word. It is embodied far more powerfully in lives lived in the Spirit of Jesus, the Spirit of him who raised Jesus from the dead.

The power of that Spirit becomes apparent when we look at the description of what fruits that Spirit brings into being in Christian lives. Paul lists them: love, joy, peace, patience, kindness, goodness, faith- fulness, gentleness, and self-control (Gal 5:22-23). A community gathered together by the Spirit of the Lord is a community of love, joy and peace. But that love, joy and peace are founded on very concrete human attitudes and commitments (virtues). They are the love, joy and peace which come into being when members of that community commit themselves to one another in patience, kindness, goodness, faithfulness, gentleness and self-control. "Being in the Spirit" is something very real, very concrete with a very clear power to communicate the meaning and power of the resurrection of Jesus in very specific ways in our lives. We can imagine what life in such a community would be like, and to the extent that we do experience this kind of community, we know the power it has for the growth of faith. This kind of community—or, perhaps more realistically, our commitment to bring this kind of community into existence—has real power to share Christian vision and experience Christian faith. For it is in this kind of community that the unfailing love of God becomes incarnate in the sacramental community gathered together by this Spirit.

From this it should be clear how important the Eucharist is for the sustenance and growth of the life of faith. The basic attitudes of our lives cannot remain unexpressed, uncelebrated. What remains unexpressed, uncelebrated soon becomes irrelevant and ceases to function in our lives. Our Christian faith is like this because it is one of our truly basic life-attitudes, the vision which shapes and interprets what it means to believe in God through Christ in the Spirit, which is what we mean when we speak of theologal or theological virtues. It needs articulation, to be brought to communal expression if it is to survive, let alone grow. And this is precisely what the Eucharist is, the celebration of the roots, the shape and the promise of the gift and grace of faith.

Likewise, it should be apparent how necessary the

reality of a living faith-community is for a real Eucharist. For this living reality, a community doing the works of faith, is what the Eucharist celebrates, and deepens. Without this, the Eucharist is a hollow and empty sign. As Paul and Aquinas stress, the reality celebrated in the Eucharist and the effect toward which the celebration of the Eucharist looks is the unity of the Church, the unity which the shared vision of faith gives us.

Mysterium fidei, the mystery of faith. Our celebration of the Eucharist brings to expression our oneness in Christ as he unites us with himself in his continuous worship of his Father and ours, binding us into the grace-filled oneness of faith in the life and power of the one Spirit.

Love and the Eucharist

Joseph M. Powers, S.J.

The life of the Christian is, in the last analysis, the fulfillment of the last testament of Jesus for those who would come to believe in him. That testament is a "new commandment" and that commandment is a commandment of love. "This is my commandment, that you love one another as I have loved you" (Jn 15:12). For the formulation of this for a Greek-speaking and Greek-reading audience, Paul and the evangelists could have used a number of Greek terms for love. They could have used the word *eros*, the wild ecstatic love in which reason is consumed by passionate frenzy. They could have used the more polite and urbane word *philia*, the love of equal for equal, of friend for friend. But they used none of these. Rather, they reached out for the word *agape*, a word of vague meaning. Generally speaking, it means the love in which the one who is loved is raised to the level of the one who loves. It designates a giving, active love, not a possessive love of self-fulfillment.

As interesting as all this philology may be, it does not really spell out in much detail the kind of love to which the follower of Jesus is called. For the commandment of love is very specifically spelled out in the Gospels. Paul stresses the fact that without Christian love, no gift or charism, no devotion or energy spent in the service of the Church is of any value at all (1 Cor 13:1-

3). And it is only when the whole life of the Christian has its roots and foundations in love that the Christian can know what the love of Christ really means (Eph 3:17-19). Later theology resumes this conviction in its statement that "charity is the form of the virtues" (e.g., *Summa Theol.* II-IIae, q. 4, a. 3). What this means concretely is that all Christian life must be some form of love, that without love as our foundation, nothing we do is of any value at all.

All though the centuries, there has been a great deal said about love, but the command of Jesus gives love its most startling human shape. The clearest and most unambiguous shape of love is the Jesus who gives his life for those he loves, the shape of the cross of Jesus. For this is the supreme act of love which Jesus makes for those whom he loves. What looks like an execution or a legal murder is actually a supreme act of love, because no one can take Jesus' life from him. Rather, he lays it down out of love (Jn 10:15-18). This is the love of Jesus, and his command is that we love one another as he has loved us, ready to lay down our lives for one another (Jn 15:13).

But this love is more than a human love. It is the love of the Father Incarnate in the life and death of Jesus. For Jesus describes his love for his own as the love of God itself: "As the Father has loved me, so I have loved you" (Jn 15:9). On Mount Horeb, God gave his name to Moses, " 'ehyeh 'aser 'ehyeh," a strange expression which is more of a promise than a name. It means "I shall be there with you; I shall be there as who I am" (J. C. Murray, *The Problem of God*, New Haven, 1963, p. 10). Now, in the death of Jesus, the meaning of that name reaches its full completion. For the faithfulness with which God has promised to be with us takes its final form in the crucified Jesus, dying for love of us. And in this sense, John can say with a staggering wealth of meaning, "God is love" (1 Jn 4:16).

Thus, we can see that the love to which we are called as Christians is not simply another kind of human love. It is to be the very incarnation of the absolutely faithful love of God, a love whose faithfulness takes its final form in Jesus' giving everything for love of us.

This command of Jesus might seem impossible. After all, who of us can love with the very faithfulness of God? Indeed, this would be an impossible command were it imposed upon us in our loneliness as individuals. But this is not the case. For the testament of Jesus comes to us through our communion with those who, in their faith, have seen and touched the Lord. "That . . . which we have seen with our own eyes . . . and touched with our own hands concerning the word of life . . . we proclaim also to you so that you may have communion with us. And our communion indeed is with the Father and with his Son, Jesus, the Christ" (1 Jn 1:1-3—my translation). It is in and out of the worshiping community that the command of love is mediated to us and that the power to live out that command is given to us.

In this light, we could read the story of Thomas as a specimen of the power of loving confessions given to those who see and touch the Lord. Jesus does not stand off from the one whose faith is weak. No, Jesus invites the believer, no matter how weak faith is, to see and touch him. And from that seeing and touching, itself a form of loving communion, there arises that startling and saving confession, "My Lord and my God" (Jn 20:28). This is a confession filled with awe—awe not so much at the majesty of the Risen Lord, but awe at the experience of seeing and touching the Lord. For this seeing and touching is an experience in which we discover within our lives a new capacity for faith, hope and love, a new capacity for living which makes of each of us a "new creation" (Gal 6:15). But, as the liturgical character of Thomas' confessions would suggest, the place for this loving and saving encounter is precisely the worshiping community.

Of course, the worshiping community is not a place where a magical transformation takes place in the lives of believers. The power which the eucharistic community has to celebrate and deepen the reality of *agape* (God's love incarnate in ours) does not somehow fall magically out of the heavens. Rather, in its Eucharist, the community celebrates the love which characterizes its life throughout all its days. It is this life of love which gives the power of living truth to celebration of the eucharistic community. For what Paul says about prophecy, tongues, martyrdom and the other gifts and callings of the Spirit is equally true of our Eucharist. We could say with him, "If I celebrated the Eucharist with every possible liturgical splendor and do not have love, it is nothing." Christian love is at the center as the power of all Christian living, and it is at the center, too, of the sacramental life in which that Christian living rises to loving expression and confession.

As a eucharistic community, then, what we celebrate most basically is our response to the command to love one another as Jesus has loved us. This is a humbling consideration because, as unlimited as is the faithfulness of the Lord in his love for us, our faithfulness is, like every other aspect of our lives, limited indeed. It is no wonder that we begin our celebration with a confession of the limited character of our faithfulness and our love. But this is no reason for discouragement, no reason to find the command of love impossible. For, as the *Constitution on the Sacred Liturgy* points out, it is Jesus himself, present in our midst, who renews his claim in the proclamation of the Gospel, and it is also Jesus himself who is present wherever two or three are gathered together in his name, responding to God's love within even the limited love which we have for one another. The love to which we are called is a gift, a gift given to us in the gift of the Spirit, and it is in the power of that Spirit, uniting us with Jesus our priest, that we can profess our love and pray for its deepening.

The works of love, joy and peace which grow out of our commitment to one another in patience, understanding, goodness, meekness and self-control (Gal 5:22-23) are the gift of the Spirit of God, the Spirit of Jesus who gives us the power to love and whose power consecrates our love as it consecrates our offering of bread and wine. The prayer of praise and thanksgiving which our Eucharist raises to God is also a prayer for the deepening of the power of his Spirit in our lives, enlarging our capacity to love and to show the works of love to one another. It is a prayer for a deepening of the love of God which has been poured into our hearts through the Holy Spirit which has been given to us (Rom 5:5). It is that Spirit which is at the heart of our power to love and to celebrate our love in the Eucharist. It is our task as Christians to open our lives as fully as possible to that presence and that power.

This, then, is the heart of the meaning of our celebration of the Eucharist: the love of God poured into our hearts through the Holy Spirit which has been given to us. The word proclaimed in the Eucharist is

basically the word of love, the love of God made manifest in the life, death and resurrection of Jesus and the
love with which we respond to his love by loving one
another. The offering we make is the offering of ourselves living out our vocation to be the incarnation of
that love for one another with the prayer that this offering, like that of bread and wine, will truly be that of the
love of Christ Incarnate in his body. Our memorial, our
proclamation of the death of the Lord until he comes, is
a recalling of the most startling and unambiguous form
of that love—Jesus' laying down his life for love of us.
Our proclamation of the mystery of faith is a cry of
faith and hope, but it is a cry of love, too. It is a cry in
which we shout out our hope to be able to grow into the
love of Christ through his Spirit at work in our lives as
a community.

This, too, is the meaning of our communion. It is
communion in the one body. It is sharing in the life of
that body as we break the one bread. It is a celebration
and pledge to share in the love which is the very spirit
which gives real life to that body. It may be that we no
longer share in the *agape* of the early Church in which
the sharing of food among the community nourished its
spirit of love as well as its bodily life. But we still share
in the one Spirit of love in a communion of love. Our
bread should taste sweet indeed as we become mindful
of what we truly eat. Our Eucharist then is at heart a
sacrament of love, the love of God poured into our
hearts through the Spirit given to us, a sacrament of the
lives of love to which we are called.

The concrete shape of the love to which we are
called is not hard to find. It is found in the fruits which
the Spirit of the Lord bears in our lives, the fruits of
faithful commitment to one another made clear in the

patience and understanding which we have for one another, in the kindness, goodness and gentleness with which we treat one another. It is out of this pattern of daily Christian living that the peace and joy of the love of God blossom in our lives (Gal 5:22-23).

But there is one aspect of God's love which we should always keep in mind when we reflect on our vocation to Christian love. God's love is not given to those who by some heroic effort have made themselves pleasing in his eyes. God does not direct his love toward those who have somehow made themselves like him, perfect, sinless. No, "God shows his love for us in that *while we were still sinners* Christ died for us" (Rom 5:8). God's love is given to those who are different from him, and he loves them precisely in their difference. This character of God's love is apparent in the love of Jesus. He begins his ministry with a quotation from Isaiah declaring that his mission is to the poor, the oppressed, the blind and the captive (Lk 4:18-19). And in his ministry, his love encompassed even the outcasts of Jewish society, "publicans and sinners" (Mt 9:9-13, 11:9, 21:31). And in the end, God shows who is his "well-beloved Son," Jesus, dying as an outcast on the cross. Perhaps one of the reasons we find the mystery of the cross so difficult to comprehend or accept is the fact that we feel that love is only possible for those who are like us. We cannot understand a love which shows itself in the service of the poor, the oppressed, the outcasts of our own society. Yet the love to which we are called as Christians, the love which we celebrate and pledge ourselves to in the celebration of our Eucharist, is precisely this love, the love of God for all, even the least acceptable.

This may be shocking for us, but as we reflect on

the meaning of our eucharistic devotion in this bicentennial era, we would do well to recall a part of the American vision which once was profoundly Christian. It is still inscribed at the base of the Statue of Liberty: "Give me your tired and your poor. . . ." Surely one aspect of the renewal is the spirit of love which is at the heart of our celebration, a love which reaches out, healing, lifting up, liberating with all the breadth and depth of God's limitless and unconditional love.

Hope and the Eucharist

Joseph M. Powers, S.J.

The first proclamation that "this Jesus whom you crucified, God has . . . raised up and made Lord and Christ" (Acts 2:22-36) was primarily a message of a new-found Christian hope. The context in which the first Christian community in Palestine experienced that the Jesus who had been crucified was not dead but alive was that of the Jewish expectation of the imminent end of history. Israel returned in joy from exile and rebuilt her temple, but the joy of return was short-lived indeed. Occupation by the Greeks and then by the Romans eroded and finally destroyed any hope that the Kingdom of God could be realized in a history which became more and more oppressive. Thus the conviction grew that the only way in which God could make his Kingdom a reality was to bring this history to a close and to initiate a completely new history, a new creation, a new world. The visions of Daniel in chapter seven and the royal Psalms nourished this piety and gave it constant expression in the life and worship of Israel. And the wildly imaginative apocalyptic literature of the time fed the popular imagination with even more explicit images for Israel's expectation.

It was to this expectation and this imagery that the first witnesses to the resurrection reached out for the proclamation of this great and final self-revelation of God. If the final act of history were to begin with the resurrection of the dead, then the fact that they experienced that God had in fact raised Jesus from the dead showed that the end was near and that soon Jesus would return in the power of the Kingdom as Lord and Christ. It was this hope which gathered the first Christian communities together, and it was this hope which gave the Church its first mission: the proclamation of the resurrection of the dead and the imminent Lordship of Jesus. We find this layer of tradition in such sayings as that of Mark 9:1: "Truly, I say to you that there are some standing here who will not taste death before they see the Kingdom of God come with power."

The posture of the Church, then, was a posture of waiting and the prayer which echoed through its eucharistic assemblies was "Maranatha"—"Come, Lord Jesus!" But the waiting went on and on. Paul's words of encouragement to the Thessalonians show the anxiety which this delay in the coming of the last days and the Kingdom caused in the Church. However something happened which began to change the shape of Christian hope. What happened was the experience of the powerful working of the Spirit in the Church. The one Spirit was experienced as the life-force and life-power in the Church. All the gifts of faith, wisdom, healing and so on were the manifestation of the power of the Spirit in the Church (1 Cor 12:4-11). All the varieties of ministries in the Church—apostles, teachers, even administrators!—are the gift of the one Spirit and the service of the one Lord (12:28). Even the Christian's capacity to pray is the gift of the Spirit (Rom 8:26-27).

Thus the shape of Christian hope underwent a change. Jesus was not simply waiting in heaven to appear as Lord and Christ at the end of the world. No, his

Lordship was experienced here and now in the life of the Church in the gifts and fruits of the Spirit. The services and ministries in the Church, the life of joy, peace, patience, understanding and commitment to one another—all this rich and complex body of experience became the medium through which Christian hope passed from the somewhat passive expectation that someday (we know not when) Jesus will come as Lord in power and glory to the more active hope that the whole pattern of Christian life was already the first fruit of the sowing of the Kingdom of God in the outpouring of the Spirit of the Risen Jesus.

Thus, Christian hope no longer simply waited for the end of time and history for the coming of God's Kingdom in glory and power. Hope flourished in this history, the history in which we live, and served as the stimulus for the Christian effort to bring that kingdom into being. The spirit of the Christian community, a spirit characterized by the fruits of the Spirit (love, joy, peace, patience, understanding, faithfulness to God and one another) was not simply significant for the character of the Christian community itself. It set the Christian community solidly in the context of history, the history of the world. The Christian hope was that through the character and quality of life of the Christian community, the proclamation of the good news and the confession that Jesus is the Lord of all history, God's Kingdom would be brought into being for every member of the human race. For it is not just the Christian community, but all creation which groans and is in labor for the birth of the children of God (Rom 8:19). The whole of the life of the Christian community was placed in hope at the service of the coming of that Kingdom of love, justice and peace (Preface: Mass of Christ the King).

This hope and the pattern of Christian conduct and concern which it enlivens are central to the community's celebration of the Eucharist. It is the realization of this hope in the lives of care and concern of the members of the community which gives power and truth to the Eucharist. It is on the basis of the frustration of this hope that Paul criticized and chided the members of the community at Corinth. For there, instead of the Eucharist being the celebration of the realization of Christian hope in the lives of its members, the rich were divided from the poor. Some went hungry in their midst and were shamed, others ate and drank to the point of drunkenness (1 Cor 1:21). Thus, those who shame the church of God and humiliate the poor (v. 22) do not celebrate the Lord's supper (v. 20). Rather, not discerning the whole community as the body, they eat and drink their own judgment, the judgment which comes not simply at the end of time, but the judgment which is present in their midst in the weak, the sick—even the dead (vv. 29-30).

Thus Paul emphasizes that this sacrament is the basis for the unity of the Church, for it is because we partake of one bread that we are one body (1 Cor 1:17). St. Thomas takes up this same conviction when he states simply that the reality which we celebrate and the effect toward which we look in our celebration of the Eucharist is the unity of the Church (*Summa Theol.* III, q. 73, a. 2, sed c). But we must be on our guard here against a rosy optimism that does not take into account all the factors which should be understood. It has been pointed out in the article "Faith and the Eucharist" (*Emmanuel* 82, May 1976) that Vatican II's *Constitution on the Sacred Liturgy* moves away from a theology of confection to a theology of celebration. What this means in our consideration of hope and the

Eucharist is that the hope of the Christian is not somehow automatically produced by the celebration of the Eucharist. Rather, that hope itself, to the extent that it has been realized in the community, must already inform the celebration of the Eucharist if our celebration is to be the celebration of something which is *true* in the worshiping community.

Thus, Paul can say that we are one body because we have partaken of the one bread. But, on the other hand, it is apparent that that unity is not an accomplished reality and he must censure the community at Corinth for not celebrating the Lord's Supper because of their divisions and neglect in the community. Paul's hope is real, based on the signs of the presence and power of the Spirit (1 Cor 12:3-13). But it is hardly a rosy optimism. Optimism is a state of mind in which we convince ourselves that things *must* get better. Often enough it really means our conviction that they cannot get worse. But this is not real or solid hope. Hope is based on those events in which the power to hope in our own and God's future is liberated by concrete experiences of the Spirit of God liberating the capacity to hope in our lives. Concretely, this means that our hope for the coming of God's Kingdom and our hope for the real forgiveness of our sinfulness are closely, *intimately tied to the quality of life* that exists in the community within which we live as Christians. If the fruits of the Spirit blossom in our community in the fidelity with which we commit ourselves to one another to be a context of patience and understanding, so that our lives may be lives of love, joy and peace, then our hope will be real indeed. If this is not true, then we are only left with an empty optimism, convincing ourselves that somehow, someday, forgiveness, love, joy and peace may become reality.

Likewise, if our hope is not real, not really liberated by the power of the fruits of the Spirit, then it is hard to see how our celebration of the Eucharist can be true as a celebration of the *pignus futurae gloriae* (the pledge of the glory which is to be). For the *power* of the Eucharist as a celebration of Christian hope depends on the *truth* with which we celebrate. Without our commitment to be a community in which the fruits of the Spirit can bloom and be shared, our symbol is empty indeed. Our celebration of the Eucharist, then, is a celebration of the reality of hope which flowers in the Christian community. But it is also, perhaps more fundamentally, a celebration of the *vocation* we all share to be and to become the one body of Christ. For the reality of Christian hope can only come about if the kind of life which liberates hope in our midst is something that we live out constantly as the essential calling we all share.

But if Christian hope is a vocation, a calling to dedicate ourselves to the flowering and fulfillment of Christian hope in the oneness of Christ's body, it is also a grace. This becomes apparent when we reflect on the character of the unity to which the eucharistic community is called. It is clear from Paul's letters that the unity to which we are called is a unity which is the fruit of the Spirit of the Lord. For it is in one Spirit that we are all baptized and we all drink of one Spirit (1 Cor 12:13). In the fruits of that Spirit, we are gathered into the community of healing, forgiveness and hope (Gal 5:22-26). But all this, as challenging as it is to the Christian community, is not what the Lord finally wishes to come into being. For in the great prayer of Jesus in the Fourth Gospel, the challenge is even more profound and startling. There, Jesus prays "for all those who believe in me through their word, that they

may be one; even as you, Father, are in me and I in
you, that they may be in us, so that the world may
believe that you have sent me" (Jn 17:20-21).

Thus, our hope in the healing, forgiveness, love,
peace and joy which come about in the community as
we pledge ourselves to one another in faithfulness, patience and understanding is basically a vocation, a calling which we are to realize by our efforts in the community. It is this calling which we celebrate in our
Eucharist, the sacrament of our hope. But far more
profoundly this hope is a grace, a calling to a oneness
which we cannot ultimately attain, but which is a gift of
the gracious and loving Father of our Lord Jesus. What
this means concretely is that although our commitment
to one another is essential for real Christian hope to
come into being, the fulfilling of our Christian vocation
to nourish one another's hope faithfully in patience and
understanding has its real depth in the fact that all this
is the gift of the Father through his Son in their Spirit.
If we can boast of the grace of hope in our community,
then we can only boast in the Lord (1 Cor 1:31).

The Eucharist, then, is the sacrament of our hope,
pignus futurae gloriae, the pledge of a glorious hope
which always lies in our future. It is the sacrament of
our striving to bring this hope into reality in the life of
every member of the Christian community and of all of
God's world. It is the sacrament in which the reality of
that hope rises to joyous expression as we experience it
growing in our lives as the power of the Spirit is mediated through our commitment to one another. As we
break the bread of life and share the cup of salvation
we taste the sweetness of this hope and nourish its
growth in our lives. But along with that sweetness we
should also taste the bitterness of our failure to nourish

one another's hope. For this hope is ultimately God's gift not only because it is a hope for a unity we cannot achieve, the unity of Father and Son in the one Spirit, but more concretely because we bear not only the Spirit of the Lord but also the spirit of sin. As faithful as we would be to one another, we fail. And our failures not only redound to ourselves, they also diminish the hopes of the community. Thus no Eucharist is perfect. It celebrates our grace, but also our sin. It celebrates our fidelity and our failing.

But God is faithful and he will not fail to bring us to that to which he has called us. In this humble but joyful hope we proclaim the death of the Lord until he comes (1 Cor 11:26).

Pastoral Office
and the Eucharist

Edward J. Kilmartin, S.J.

What is the Church's understanding of the offices of bishop and presbyter and their relationship to the Eucharist? Within Catholic school theology for many centuries the answers to these questions have been sought mainly in decrees of ecumenical councils, extra-conciliar decisions of Roman pontiffs, and the teaching of ranking theologians. Liturgical rites and texts have been frequently used to support theological positions already established in a way similar to the use of New Testament "proof texts." On the whole, the liturgical witness was only theoretically recognized as a true source of theology from which new insights might be derived in order to deepen the theology of pastoral office.

This situation has changed in recent years. Catholic theologians and the Magisterium are more sensitive to the uniqueness of the liturgy as a true source of theology. It is recognized that every human experience reaches its full expression by way of symbolic action and word and that this is true of the life of faith. The liturgy, being a celebration of the life of faith, is understood to express the faith in a way which surpasses any particular formulations of the teaching office of the Church or theologians. Hence to adequately answer the question initially posed, modern Catholic theologians are paying more attention to the liturgies of ordination and the Eucharist.

The understanding of pastoral office and its relationship to the Eucharist expressed in these sources provides an indispensable ground for evaluating the later relevant decrees of the Magisterium and the teaching of theologians. These latter sources are derived from reflection on authentic Christian life, including the liturgical life. Consequently they need to be continually integrated into the more comprehensive liturgical tradition in order to avoid too narrow a perspective on, and to promote a deepening of the understanding of, the pastoral office.

However we cannot arbitrarily choose our liturgical sources. Rather we should employ those which reach back to the times of liturgical origins in the East and West. In the beginning of its liturgical life, the Christian faith expressed itself more simply and spontaneously. The symbolic actions and prayers were a more direct mirror image of the life of faith. The clarity of intention was not impeded by purely ceremonial rites and secondary theological reflections which found a place in the course of the evolution of sacramental rites.

From these origins we can trace the genuine stream of the liturgical tradition of East and West. Hence we are better able to judge to what extent later local verbal and gestural additions and the theology reflected in them are in agreement with the authentic ecclesial whole tradition. This method was used by Pius XII in the Apostolic Constitution *Sacramentum Ordinis* to determine, for the future, the essential gesture of the rite of ordination of priesthood. In view of the fact that the handing over of the cup and paten *(traditio instrumentorum)* proved to be a late addition of ecclesiastical origin, he was able to award it, at least for the future, a purely ceremonial value and to affirm the essential gesture to be the laying on of hands.

What do we learn from the earliest ordination rites and eucharistic liturgies about the nature of the offices of bishop and presbyter and their relation to the Eucharist? Before answering this question we must say something about the sources to be used. First of all, the important eucharistic prayers in the great churches of the East and West are close variations of formulations derived from the fourth century. They reflect a unified tradition which is already found in the early third-century text of the *Apostolic Tradition* of Hippolytus. The eucharistic prayer of this document relates to an earlier tradition as some second-century sources (Justin and Irenaeus) indicate.

Secondly, the ordination prayers of the Byzantine liturgy and the pure Roman rite can be traced to the fifth century. So in this instance our sources are not as ancient as those of the Eucharist. Nevertheless the ordination rites of the *Apostolic Tradition*, in essential aspects, stand in continuity with those of the old *Roman Sacramentaries* and the Oriental ordination liturgies. In this connection it is noteworthy that in the new *Pontificale Romanum*, promulgated by Paul VI in 1968, the episcopal ordination prayer stemming from the fifth century was replaced by that of the *Apostolic Tradition* (which is also used up to the present in the Coptic and West Syrian liturgies).

In view of the above considerations, we are justified in taking the *Apostolic Tradition* as our point of departure. The eucharistic prayer found here offers a key to the understanding of the fourth-century eu-

charistic prayers of both East and West. Its ordination
prayers afford the most direct access to the understanding of the ordination rites of the East and the old
Roman Sacramentaries.

We will first show how the eucharistic celebration
reveals the degrees and functions of ecclesiastical offices and their relation to the whole community (especially in the eucharistic celebration). Afterward we will
consider the ordination rites in the same way. As an aid
to the reader an appendix has been added to this essay
containing the eucharistic prayer of *Apostolic Tradition*
and key passages of its ordination prayers of bishop
and presbyter.

In the eucharistic rite of the *Apostolic Tradition*
the whole community presents its gifts of bread and
wine. The whole community as such offers and gives
thanks. It accomplishes the memorial of the Lord and
is built up by sharing the eucharistic gifts which become
the body and blood of Christ in the liturgical presentation through the work of the Holy Spirit. However,
within the rite, the deacons act as intermediaries between the people and the bishop together with his presbyters. The deacons bring the gifts of bread and wine to
the bishop. The role of leadership of the Eucharist falls
to the bishop with his presbyters: bishop and presbyters
place hands over the bread and wine in a sacrificial gesture. However the dominant role of the bishop is manifested by the fact that he alone speaks the eucharistic
prayer and is personally assisted by the deacons who
bring the bread and wine to him at the outset and assist
him at the distribution of communion.

In this rite the bishop and presbyters exercise a
pastoral leadership. When Hippolytus describes the efficacy of the bishop's prayer in the section dealing with

the Paschal Mass after baptism, he simply states that the bishop "eucharistizes" the bread and wine that they may be "antitypes" of the body and blood of Christ. In his view, the prayer of the bishop, which is made in the name of the community, coincides with the work of the Spirit who (in the language of the fourth century) "changes" *(metapoiein)* or "transforms" *(transformare)* the elements.

The ordination prayer for the rite of episcopal ordination of the *Apostolic Tradition* confirms the view that the bishop's role in the Eucharist is understood to be an exercise of the pastoral office. In the decisive section of this prayer the petition is made that the bishop-elect be given the "princely Spirit" and the grace to "feed your holy flock." As representative functions of this pastoral office the offering of "the gifts of your holy Church" and "the authority to remit sins" are mentioned. These sacramental functions thus appear to follow from the nature of the pastoral office in a "holy Church," i.e., permeated by the Spirit in all its essential structures.

The content and structure of the eucharistic prayer of the *Apostolic Tradition* and those of the fourth century reflect the same concept of office and its priestly functions—i.e., priestly functions derive from the pastoral office in a sacramentally structured Church (= a Church permeated by the Spirit). The eucharistic prayer of the *Apostolic Tradition* and the Byzantine anaphoras of Basil and Chrysostom show a close resemblance in the way the proclamation of the history of salvation in the thanksgiving section incorporates the account of the institution of the Eucharist. In these texts the structure does not allow the account of the institution of the Eucharist to be considered as an isolated "form of consecration of the elements." Rather the act of Christ at the Last Supper is mentioned as an important part of the history of salvation for which we give thanks. What is praised as an act of Christ relating to the whole economy of salvation is understood to become a sacramental reality in the celebration by the liturgical presentation of the community of believers under the leadership of the bishop through the cooperation of the Spirit who is invoked.

The liturgical act of the community by which the memorial of the Last Supper becomes a sacramental reality and the indispensable role of the Spirit, in whom alone it can take place, are expressed in the *anamnesis* and the *epiclesis*. The anamnesis of the *Apostolic·Tradition*, which follows the thanksgiving prayer, states: "Therefore recalling his death and resurrection, we offer to you the bread and the cup. . . ." A slight variant of this prayer is found in the Byzantine and Roman eucharistic prayers. It refers to the offering of the bread and wine in obedience to the command of Christ and is, as in the case of Jesus at the Last Supper, a symbol of the offering of the believers themselves in union with their Lord.

But since the bread and wine become the body and blood of Christ only through the work of the Spirit, the prayer of the *Apostolic Tradition* adds the *epiclesis*, the invocation of the Father to send the Holy Spirit to sanctify "the oblation of the holy Church." The belief that the elements become the body and blood through the work of the Spirit, implicit in the text of the *Apostolic Tradition*, is made explicit in the *epiclesis* of the Byzantine liturgies. A variant of this epiclesis is also found in the *Supplices te rogamus* of the old Roman Canon. Here the divine action over the gifts is depicted as involving the special ministry of the angels who bear the gifts to "your altar on high in order that we, who receive the most holy body and blood of your Son by participation from this altar, may be filled with every heavenly blessing and grace."

The genuine liturgical tradition concerning the function of office in the Eucharist is accessible in these eucharistic texts and actions. The office-bearer has the task of eucharistic leadership, especially the speaking of the eucharistic prayer. This prayer is both a proclamation of the history of salvation *(thanksgiving)* and a prophetic preaching: the announcement of the efficacious saving action of God in Christ as present in the celebration *(epiclesis)*. The symbolic action basic to this preaching is the offering of the bread and wine as expression of the self-offering of the community, by which the command of Christ is fulfilled *(anamnesis)*. In the liturgical presentation of the gifts of the Spirit-filled Church, the gifts become the body and blood of Christ through the work of the Spirit and so serve to deepen the unity of the one body in the eucharistic eating and drinking.

The requirement of pastoral office for the celebration of the Eucharist is indicated in the ordination prayer of the bishop which describes the eucharistic leadership as a function of the episcopacy. It is also expressed in the consistent connection made between ordination to the pastoral office and the concrete celebration of the Eucharist. Beginning with the *Apostolic Tradition* we find that the bishop always celebrates the Eucharist immediately after his ordination. The same holds true for the presbyter. In the tradition of the East and West, immediately after ordination, the presbyter concelebrates with the bishop as his first pastoral act.

While the liturgy of ordination shows that the leadership of the Eucharist belongs to the pastoral office, it also indicates *why* this should be so. In the ordination rite of bishop of the *Apostolic Tradition*, the laying on of hands signifies not only the mediation of the gift of the Spirit for the exercise of pastoral office but also the continuity of this office with the apostolic office instituted by Christ the head of the Church which lives from his Spirit. This is expressed in the petition: "And now pour forth on this elect the power which is from you, the princely Spirit, which you gave to your beloved child Jesus Christ, which he himself gave to the holy Apostles who established the Church in every place. . . ." Thus this ordination bestows a commission with a view to building up the Church which has Christ for its capstone and the apostles as foundation (Eph 2:20).

The connection between ordination to the pastoral office and the celebration of the Eucharist affirms that the office of bishop is realized most directly in carrying out the celebration in which the Lord builds up his Church by uniting it with his saving worship and communicating with it through his sacramental body and blood. Thus the ordering of pastoral office and Eucharist springs from the roots of the Church's essential structures. It corresponds to the New Testament statements about the building up of the Church as a body through the Eucharist (1 Cor 10:16-17) and the function of pastors "to build up the body of Christ" (Eph 4:12).

The inner unity of the governing, preaching and sacramental functions of the bishop's office holds also for the presbyter. In the rite of ordination for presbyters of the *Apostolic Tradition*, the petition is made that the candidate receive "the Spirit of grace and

counsel of the presbyterate in order that he may aid and
govern your people. . . ." The presbyter, ordained as
counselor and co-worker of the bishop, shares in the
leadership of the local church. He also exercises liturgical leadership by which the Church is built up. In this
matter Hippolytus makes only one exception when he
describes the ordination of deacons: the presbyter cannot "ordain a cleric." This liturgical role of the presbyter flows from the essence of the pastoral office. It is
not mentioned in the ordination prayer of the presbyter
because it is understood to be one of the functions of
the pastoral office.

The same concept of presbyteral office is found in
the old *Roman Sacramentaries* where the presbyteral
ordination prayer, linked with the imposition of hands,
refers to the presbyter as *cooperator* of the episcopal
office and *praedicator* of the second rank. Here again
the priestly functions are not mentioned. They are understood to be included in the commission to the pastoral office.

The Byzantine liturgy has an ordination prayer,
linked with the laying on of hands, which is comparable
to the Roman prayer of the fifth century. But in this
rite the relationship of the two pastoral offices to the
eucharistic celebration is well expressed by the way in
which the ordinations are inserted into the flow of the
whole eucharistic liturgy. The bishop is ordained before
the beginning of the liturgy of the word, after the small
entrance with the Gospel book; the presbyter is ordained before the beginning of the eucharistic liturgy,
after the solemn bringing forth of the gifts of the great
entrance. We may note also that the deacon is ordained
after the anaphora, before the beginning of the Communion rite, since he is ordained not to exercise leader-

ship of the eucharistic celebration but to assist in the distribution of Holy Communion.

Conclusions

Christ instituted the pastoral office as a means of building up his Church. Within the functions of the pastoral office is included the leadership of the liturgy of the Eucharist, derived also from Christ, which is an important means of building up the Church.

This understanding of the early Church was spontaneously expressed in the rite of ordination of the bishop and in his role in the celebration of the Eucharist. The ordination rite of presbyter also indicates that the candidate receives a share in the pastoral office. His leadership role in the Eucharist is first manifested by the act of placing hands over the bread and wine together with the bishop in the eucharistic celebration which follows his ordination to the presbyterate.

The ordination rites of bishop and presbyter are a mirror image of the nature of these offices and their special relation to the celebrations of the faith of the Church permeated by the Spirit, at the summit of which is the Eucharist. Consequently any devaluation of the rite of ordination to the pastoral office by any Christian denomination presents a serious hindrance to the recognition of the pastoral office of those communities by churches which have retained the genuine whole liturgical tradition. On the other hand, possible earlier ruptures of pastoral succession in Christian communities due to the omission of the laying on of hands and the appropriate prayer made by a qualified pastor, or to some other more basic defect in the liturgical presentation of the meaning of pastoral office, do not necessarily imply a subsequent lack of pastoral office in these communities.

If the word of God is preached and the liturgy celebrated in such a way that the community is built up, one cannot simply speak of "invalid official acts" as though they had no meaning. In these cases the existence of a pastoral office is proved by the results.

However, if the traditional meaning of pastoral office is not expressed liturgically through the ordination rites and in the mode of celebration of the Eucharist, the consciousness of a unity of faith between such communities and the Roman Catholic Church—a unity of faith which can represent itself in a communal eucharistic celebration—is not yet realizable. Where Christians are faithful to the original structures of the apostolic Church and express this liturgically, as is the case with the Orthodox Church, the situation is different. Thus in this case Vatican II was able to decide: ". . . given suitable circumstances and the approval of Church authority, some worship is not merely possible but recommended" (*Decree on Ecumenism*, n. 15), and the *Directory on Ecumenism* of the Secretariat for the Promotion of Christian Unity understood this to include "eucharistic" worship (n. 40).

I
EUCHARISTIC PRAYER OF HIPPOLYTUS

Thanksgiving Section

We thank you, God, through your beloved child Jesus Christ whom you sent to us in the final times as redeemer and messenger of your plan; who is your

Word inseparable through whom you made all and, in your good pleasure, you sent from heaven into the womb of the virgin; and who, conceived within her, was made flesh and was manifested as your Son, born of the Holy Spirit and the virgin; who, fulfilling your will and acquiring for you a holy people, extended hands while he suffered, in order to free from suffering those who believed in you; who, when he was handed over to voluntary suffering, in order to destroy death and break the chains of the devil, and crush the netherworld and illumine the just, and fix the limit and manifest the resurrection, taking bread, giving thanks to you, he said: Take, eat, this is my body which is broken for you. And likewise the cup, saying: This is my blood, which is shed for you. When you do this, you make my memorial.

Liturgical Presentation

Therefore recalling his death and resurrection, we offer to you the bread and cup, thanking you because you have made us worthy to stand before you and minister to you.

Epiclesis

And we ask that you send your Holy Spirit on the oblation of the holy Church; gathering into one, give to all who participate of the sacred (mysteries) to be filled with the Holy Spirit for the confirmation of the faith in truth in order that we may praise and glorify you through your child Jesus Christ: through whom be glory and honor to you, Father and Son and Holy

Spirit, in your holy Church both now and in the ages of ages. Amen.

II
KEY PASSAGE OF EPISCOPAL ORDINATION PRAYER

And now pour forth on this elect the power which is from you, the princely Spirit, which you gave to your beloved child Jesus Christ, which he himself gave to the holy Apostles, who established the Church in every place as your sanctuary for the glory and unfailing praise of your name. Grant, Father, who knows hearts, to this your servant, whom you have chosen for the episcopate, that he may feed your holy flock and exercise the high priesthood before you without reproach, serving you night and day, that he may ceaselessly propitiate your countenance and offer the gifts of your holy Church, that he may have by the Spirit of the high priesthood the authority to remit sins according to your commandment.

III
KEY PASSAGE OF PRESBYTERAL ORDINATION PRAYER

God and Father of our Lord Jesus Christ, look on this your servant and accord to him the Spirit of grace and counsel of the presbyterate in order that he may aid and govern your people with a pure heart, as you looked on the people of your election and commanded Moses to choose presbyters whom you filled with your Spirit which you granted to your minister.

The Basis of the
Sunday Mass Obligation

Edward J. Kilmartin, S.J.

I

A few New Testament texts refer to the regular assemblies of Christians of local churches. They are described as a "coming together"[1] or an "assembling together."[2] Paul's remark "If the whole church gathers in the place . . ."[3] is equivalent to "the full assembly of the local church." The Epistle to the Hebrews alludes to the responsibility of Christians to support one another through regular assemblies: ". . . not neglecting to assemble together, as is the habit of some, but encouraging one another. . . ."[4]

One of the main reasons for such gatherings was communal worship.[5] At an early period, at least in some parts of the Church, the first day of the week was designated for the meeting.[6] This choice must be explained as a consequence of the fact that Christ made it a privileged day through his appearances to his followers after his death.[7] Through the resurrection appearances on the first day of the week Christ made himself personally present to the chosen witnesses. He created their faith in his victory over death and in his abiding presence sharing the grace of salvation with them. Thus the resurrection appearances made the first day of the week the new day of salvation: a holy day to be observed by Christians in joyful remembrance of the salvation obtained through Christ. In a relatively short time, in some local churches, the term "first day" was supplanted by "the Lord's Day,"[8] or simply by "the Lord's."[9]

In Acts 20:7 we read that the purpose of the gathering on the first day of the week was "to break bread": "On the first day of the week when we had met to break bread. . . ." While some discussion still goes on about the precise meaning of the "breaking of bread," it seems almost certain that the phrase should be identified with the Lord's Supper of 1 Corinthians 11:20.

II

Early in the post-apostolic period we find evidence that the observance of Sunday as a holy day was explicitly connected with the day of the resurrection of Christ. Ignatius of Antioch (d. A.D. 110) says that Christians are distinguished from Jews in that they orient their lives on the Lord's Day: ". . . no longer living for the Sabbath, but for the Lord's [Day], on which our life sprang up through him and his death . . . and by this mystery we received faith."[10] The Epistle of Barnabas (c. A.D. 130) states that Christians celebrate Sunday, "the eighth day," because Christ rose on that day and so inaugurated the new age.[11]

In the second century the belonging together of the "Lord's Day" and the "Lord's Supper" is self-evident. On the Day of the Lord, who works in the assembled community, the distinctive mode of celebration could be none other than the Eucharist. Justin Martyr (c.

A.D. 150) takes for granted that the Eucharist is celebrated on Sunday by all Christians: "On the day called of the sun an assembly is made in one place by all dwelling either in the cities or in the countryside."[12]

Ignatius of Antioch alludes to the Christian obligation to attend eucharistic assemblies: "Seek then to come together more frequently to give thanks and glory to God."[13] Moreover he judges the failure to join the assemblies as a sign of weakness or loss of faith: "So then whoever does not come to the place is possessed of pride, and has separated himself."[14]

The recognition of the responsibility to assemble for Christian worship derives from the consciousness which Christians had of being a community called to worship God in the Spirit of Christ, to support one another's faith and to deepen its union with God through the hearing of the word of God and eucharistic communion. The explicit formulation of this understanding is found in the Syrian *Didascalia* (c. A.D. 250). The anonymous author, a bishop, gives this instruction to fellow bishops:

> Now when you teach, command and warn the people to be constant in assembling in the church and not to withdraw themselves but always assemble, lest any man diminish the church by not assembling, and cause the body of Christ to be short of a member.

As a model example for the bishop's instruction of his people, the author adds:

> Since therefore you are the members of Christ, do not scatter yourselves from the church by not as-

sembling. Seeing that you have Christ for your head, as he promised—for you are partakers with us—be not neglectful of yourselves, and deprive not our Savior of his member, and do not rend or scatter his body. . . . On the Lord's Day leave everything and run eagerly to your church; for she is your glory. Otherwise what excuse have they before God who do not assemble on the Lord's Day to hear the word of life and be nourished with the divine food which abides forever.[15]

Thus the author recognized that the body of Christ lives from Christ the head. Consequently he teaches that all members are required to share in the common assembly which affords communion with Christ by word and Eucharist.

What we have been saying about the origin of the Sunday Eucharist and the Christian understanding of the grounds and responsibility for regular attendance is summarized in Vatican II's *Constitution on the Sacred Liturgy:*

By an apostolic tradition which took its origin from the very day of Christ's resurrection, the Church celebrates the paschal mystery every eighth day; with good reason then, this bears the name of the Lord's Day or the Day of the Lord. For on this day Christ's faithful should come together into one place so that, hearing the word of God and taking part in the Eucharist, they may call to mind the passion, the resurrection, and the glorification of the Lord Jesus, and may thank God who "has begotten us again, through the resurrection of Jesus Christ from the dead unto a living hope" (1

Pet 1:13). Hence the Lord's Day is the original feast day, and it should be proposed to the piety of the faithful and taught to them in such a way that it may become in fact a day of joy and of freedom from work.[16]

This text traces the Sunday feast to an apostolic tradition motivated by a desire to single out the recurring day of the resurrection of Jesus Christ as the day on which to celebrate the mystery of redemption. It implies that by an apostolic tradition the Lord's Supper was the distinctive mark of this day. Hence it concludes that the faithful should observe this feast through the Sunday Eucharist. The grounds for this observation is not merely the tradition but the meaning of the Eucharist: the celebration òf the paschal mystery. The text does not dwell on the obligatory nature of the weekly gathering. Rather it stresses the obligation of the pastors to instruct the faithful about the meaning of the Eucharist in such a way that they may be led to a joyful participation.

III

The first canonical legislation concerning attendance at the Sunday Eucharist is found at the beginning of the fourth century. The Council of Elvira (c. A.D. 309), in canon 21, states:

If anyone located in the city does not attend church three Sundays, let him abstain (i.e., from eucharistic communion) in order that he may be seen to be rebuked.

This canon presupposes that an obligation exists to share in Sunday Eucharist. It does not establish a law. It merely applies a sanction to those who do not observe a practice which is rooted in the nature of Christian life and which cannot be neglected for a long time (three weeks!) without serious consequences for the individual's life of faith.

A contemporary document affords a valuable witness for this understanding of the Christian obligation to participate in the weekly assembly: *The Acts of the Martyrs Saturninus, Dativus and Their Companions*.[17] These Christians belonged to the small congregation of the town of Abitina which was located about 150 miles from Carthage in the upper valley of the Mejerda River. Sometime after February 23, 303, when Diocletian had· signed the edict outlawing the Christian Church, the bishop of this church had submitted to the precept and handed over the Scriptures to officials. The community rejected him and continued to meet under the leadership of the presbyter Saturninus. When their activity became known to Roman authorities they were brought to Carthage for trial.

During the interrogation by the proconsul, Saturninus was asked whether he had participated in Christian assemblies: a crime punishable by death. The following exchange then took place:

S. I am the instigator in whose house assemblies took place.

PC. Why have you acted against the precept, Saturninus?

S. The *dominicum* cannot be neglected. Thus the law commands.

Later, while under torture, Saturninus was asked by the proconsul: "Why did you act against the precept?" He answered: "Thus the law commands, thus the law teaches." Commenting on this response, the text adds: "O quite admirable and divine response of the proclaiming presbyter-doctor. Even under torture the presbyter proclaims the most holy law in behalf of which he has willingly undergone suffering."[18]

The interrogation of the lector Emeritus then follows:

PC. Did assemblies take place in your house against the precepts of the Emperor?

E. In my house we observed the *dominicum*.

PC. Why did you allow these to enter?

E. Because they are my brothers, and I was not able to prevent them.

PC. But you ought to have prevented them.

E. I was unable because we cannot be without the *dominicum*.[19]

After this episode another Christian, Felix, is asked about his attendance at assemblies. He responds simply that he is a Christian. At this point all the confessors exclaim: "We are Christians; we cannot but observe the holy law of the Lord to the shedding of blood." Ignoring this interruption, the proconsul addresses Felix again: "I do not ask whether you are a Christian, but did you participate in assemblies, or have you any writings?" The text continues with this comment on the proconsul's statement:

O stupid and laughable interrogation of the judge. He says: "Be silent as to whether you are a Christian. And adds: "Were you in the assemblies? Respond!" As though a Christian could be without the *dominicum* or the *dominicum* be celebrated without the Christian. Do you not know, Satan, the Christian is constituted in the *dominicum* and the *dominicum* in the Christian, so that the one without the other does not stand.[20]

In this text *dominicum* (the Lord's) refers directly to the eucharistic assembly: the name derives from the Lord's Day on which it takes place.[21] This usage was current in North Africa and Rome in the third and fourth centuries.[22] Thus the eucharistic assemblies are related to a *law*: the holy law of the Lord. This should not be understood as a positive law of the Lord about the holiness of Sunday. Rather what is meant is the *law of the Gospel*: the spirit of the Gospel which, in a comprehensive way, calls for the celebration of the Lord's Day through the Eucharist. This observance is referred to the law of Christ himself, and the practical observance of it is viewed as the distinctive mark of being a Christian: of belonging to Christ, and a necessity for the continued belonging to Christ.

IV

Up to the fourth century we encounter only warnings and instructions about Sunday attendance. The later positive law obligation is repeated in the Code of Canon Law, canon 1248. This positive law affirms the value of the custom which took its origin from the relationship of the Christian life to the Eucharist. However it is often interpreted as an obligation which derives from the will of the law-giver and not from the implications of the Eucharist for the life of faith of the community and the individual as such. In this perspective often enough the appeal is made to the natural law obligation of a community of like-minded believers to worship God together and to the human need of the community to express its faith regularly in order to keep it alive. To this corresponds the responsibility of the members to cooperate and the authority of the Church leaders to specify the way and the times for fulfilling this obligation and need.

This approach, which is insensitive to the experience underlying the primitive custom of a regular Sunday Eucharist, can give the impression that the choice of the Eucharist as the distinctive mark of the obligatory assemblies is arbitrary. It gives rise to the question: Why do we not substitute some other service from time to time?

It is important for pastors to stress the fact that the Sunday Mass obligation is not based on grounds independent of the meaning of the Eucharist, but on the need of the faith to express itself eucharistically. If Church law is to make any sense theologically in this regard, it must be interpreted as affirming the positive value of the Eucharist.

The Church's understanding in faith of the meaning of the Sunday Eucharist is the basis for the obligation of Church authorities to insist on this practice. Correlative to this, the individual's obligation to attend is ultimately grounded also in the recognition of the meaning of the Eucharist for furthering the life of faith and not on a positive law of the Church. To comply with the positive law simply because it is commanded, and not because of the basis of the law, places the act outside the scope of the life of faith. In the measure that this obligation is explained simply as a law of the Church which must be obeyed, the impression is given that it is an extra burden without direct reference to the life of faith or even a "good work" which substitutes for the response of faith. However, either the Sunday Eucharist obligation derives from its peculiar role in the life of faith or it is no obligation at all. Consequently it places no new obligation on believers which lies outside the scope of the faith.

This consideration points to the responsibility of pastors to so instruct the individual's faith, and so celebrate the Eucharist, that the conditions for a fruitful participation of the believers may be present. It is important that this Church law be recognized for what it is. It is not something imposed from outside but takes its origin from the meaning of the Eucharist. Christians should be urged to attend Sunday Eucharist not through threat of sanction but through the *catechesis* of the meaning of the Eucharist for their life of faith as the quotation from Vatican II's *Constitution on the Sacred Liturgy* makes clear.

NOTES

1. 1 Cor 11:17, 18, 20, 33, 34.
2. Heb 10:25.
3. 1 Cor 14:23.
4. Heb 10:25.
5. Acts 2:42, 47; Eph 5:19-20.
6. Acts 20:7; 1 Cor 16:2.
7. Jn 20:19, 26; also possibly Jn 21:3.
8. Rev 1:10.

9. *Didache* 14:1; Ignatius of Antioch, *Ep. to Magnesians* 9.1.

10. *Loc. cit.*

11. 15.8; For similar remarks, cf. Justin Martyr, *1 Apology* 67; *Dialogue with Trypho* 41.

12. *1 Apology* 67.

13. *Ep. to Ephesians* 13.1. The context indicates a eucharistic setting.

14. *Ep. to Ephesians* 5.3. Here again the context indicates a eucharistic setting.

15. R. H. Connolly, *Didascalia Apostolorum* (Oxford, 1929), ch. XIII, p. 124.

16. No. 106.

17. T. Ruinart, *Acta martyrum Saturnini, Dativi et aliorum plurimorum martyrum in Africa.* PL 8, pp. 705-713.

18. *Ibid.*, no. X, p. 710.

19. *Ibid.*, no. XI, pp. 710-711.

20. *Ibid.*, no. XII, pp. 711-712.

21. In the commentary on the proconsul's statement to Felix, *assembly* is equated with *dominicum*.

22. When referring to the nature of the eucharistic celebration, dominicum is generally qualified. Thus Cyprian speaks of the *dominical sacrifice: sacrificium dominicum . . . celebrari* (Ep. 63.9).

The Eucharist and Secular Man

George McCauley, S.J.

Sanctuary: A place where they cannot come and get you. An inviolate space carved out of the world yet in it. A stillness buttressed by stone walls. A claim to be doing something so radically different from secular pursuits that it should be left alone. A distancing. People staring at the bread and the cup and the intense, flickering light. Even the painted onlookers at the windows are focused inward. From the outside world they are hardly discernible, like spoiled smudges on indifferent glass.

Long tradition places our Eucharist in this sanctuary. So we might ask what the Eucharist has to do with the world outside. This question can be replayed in many keys: Should there be politics in the pulpit? Should profane music resound in the churches? Should collections for various practical causes be taken up? Should the host be replaced by Wonder Bread? Should liturgical communities be based on job or ethnic or educational groupings? Should normal dress replace the elaborate costuming? Should storefront churches proliferate? Should lectors be judged on their ability to use a microphone rather than on their generosity and sincerity? Should the art, the banners, the architecture reflect the City of God or the city of man?

The ambivalence that we feel concerning the relationship of our Eucharist to the world is reflected in John's gospel version of the Last Supper. What did that Supper have to do with the world? We find that Jesus suffers a similar ambivalence as he tries to relate the events of the upper room to the world outside it.

Indeed, John presents Jesus as suffering these conflicts throughout his career: The world is a famished place, ready for the scrap heap, so he must nourish it (6:33, 51) and salvage it (3:17; 4:42; 12:47). The world is nice to its own kind, which, alas, includes some of his closest friends (7:7). It knows only what it wants to know, which does not include him (1:10). It is capable of little more than passing enthusiasms (12:19), yet it wants to be at the hub of things (7:4). It is the place where Bossism rules (12:31). The world is a hateful place that one should not reasonably want to be around (12:25). Jesus feels as foreign to it as though he arrived on the scene from another planet (1:9; 3:19; 8:23), as though the landmarks should have been more familiar but do not fit happy memories or hopes for it (1:10).

He has, therefore, a lot of prophetic advice for the world (6:14). He will be the ambassador to it of another vision of things (10:36; 12:27), in particular that God his Father is love (3:16). While remaining non-judgmental (3:17; 12:47), he certainly maintains that he is going to reverse the world's standards of who knows what (9:39). In the presence of love Bossism is out (12:31). Yet, so much does he sense that what he hears from the Father (8:26) is at variance with the world that he feels like the one bright spot in the gloom (3:19; 8:12), like a beacon to others in the dark (11:9; 12:46). He will try to share his views with others and to get them to share in his work. But he is aware that they themselves may be in collusion with the world and its standards (8:23). In any case, even if alone (as he apparently often feels), he will attempt to dispose of the sin in the world for good (1:29).

These themes recur with greater insistence in John's account of the Last Supper. For Jesus, the world is coming to an end, but the ironies around this fact pile up: It is ending for him because he is leaving it (13:1; 16:20), but his leaving it is not a simple statement of fact. It is the logical outcome of his conflict with the world, and we might wonder whether he thought his leaving it was a triumphant exit or a regrettable fiasco, as he falls victim to the powerful Bosses (14:30). Just as the Father sent him, so the world sends him back with its opinion of him clearly attached to the corpse. Yet, in dispatching him its ways are finally going to be shown up. While he is coming to his end, so is it. *It is going to have to face the truth* (14:17), namely, that Jesus was right all along: its way is to kill love wherever that love threatens its power.

But even at the last Jesus has to admit that the world may not recognize this turn of events, because it does not love him (14:19, 22). Those who do love him will recognize what it was all about when he is gone. They will know what kind of God the Father is (17:6, 24) because they will have seen the tenacity of Jesus' love. In that moment they will find true peace and not the phony peace which the world would define as knuckling under to the powers that be. Yet Jesus is not entirely without skepticism about his friends (16:32). He worries about them now that the world does not consider them its own kind (15:18-19; 17:11, 14). Realistically, they will be in the world (17:15); in fact he sends them there (17:18). But they are going to need courage, so he, the convicted one, tells them that he has won his case over the world (16:33). They are going to need a lawyer, in fact, so he promises someone who will carry on the argument with the world for them (16:8).

The final irony is that his disciples are sad to learn the ways of real love, while the world, which should have been happy to get rid of him, now can be happy to have discovered the source of its own sadness (16:20). The only analogy that leaps to his mind to explain all this pain is that of the pain preceding the birth of a human being into the world (16:21). Despite itself, the world is going to be what it wants to be, a human place. But Jesus, too, feels the pain. He feels dishonored by it all (17:5). He seems almost vindictive toward the world (17:9). Still, he will consecrate himself to his task (17:19).

So the Last Supper, by John's account, seems to be a seesaw event for Jesus. Hopes, convictions, fears, resentments, memories, and strongly felt alliances all pass through his mind with almost convulsive irregularity, and all are the stuff of the decision of fidelity that he makes at that meal. Biblical historians force us to ask whether John's picture of Jesus' emotion-laden and wavering attitude toward the world at the Last Supper represents what really happened there. Or does it, they ask, correspond to a subsequent perception of him, a pious one to be sure, but a frankly subjective one which reflects rather the history of John's (or his community's) experience with the world?

To answer this question would require an impossibly long discussion of what is meant by "what really happened" and of the canons for "historically" determining this. We certainly do not wish to substitute faith (still less credulity) for historical propriety. But we are often put in an unfair bind. On the one hand, the canons of historical precision have little patience with imagining (beyond what we "know" historically) the psychology of Jesus. On the other hand, some practitioners of biblical history are slow to discuss how they integrate what we "know" historically with what we "know" of people from the dull predictability of the human condition. Yet, in countless ways historians draw on this latter knowledge to establish many of the "known" facts of history. On the basis of this knowledge of people in general, for instance, they estimate the credibility of credulousness of writers, the likelihood of influences on them, the plausibility of information passing from one source to another, the probability of the accuracy of that information, and so on. Throughout they claim to be doing history, and they would justly resent their work being called an exercise in imagining the past.

So we need not apologize if we take John's account as historical in the sense that it captures with likelihood the experience of such a man from such a background faced with such a turn of events. To assume that John is trying to express his own experience of Jesus rather than to capture historically something of Jesus' own experience is arbitrary in the extreme. Even if words are added by him to flesh out the account of Jesus' experience, to call his account of the experience unhistorical because of the words is to prejudice the matter hopelessly. We have to ask whether the psychology of Jesus might be such a threatening topic to us all that we conveniently cut off what historical access we do have to it.

Even apart from this biblical debate, we have the tie between Jesus' humanity and our own to explore.

We realize that we are most really present at moments of hard decision. Any action we take will now bear the unmistakable stamp of our freedom on it. Our laborious choices about the world immediately expose us to reaction, conflict, and judgment, and the more so the more deliberately we have acted. Moreover, our real presence is a matter of real drama, not only in the sense that we have made a decision rather than not made one, but also in the sense that our choices are made in love or in hate. By them we can remake the world as a good place or fashion it in some morose image of our worst self. Again, this drama never takes place without certain props. Our key decisions are accompanied by some scenario, each with its own etiquette: it was when I was walking home that night; it was after the argument over our son; it was when I looked up at the doctor; it was at the fountain; it was when she handed me the clipping.

With this understanding of our own hard decisions, why, then, do we find it so difficult to see Jesus experiencing something like this at the Last Supper? The components are there. He has to estimate the course of events that, as any astute observer of people could judge, are leading him to his death. His time has run out. His team seems hopeless. The upper room—and this is most pertinent to our topic—is filled with input and overflow from events outside the room. Past associations are there, the memory of enemies, of dropouts, the long speeches leading who knows where, the ungrateful healed, the silently convinced, the work undone. Every face at the table recalls some incident of almost success, of slow progress, of strained learning, of confusion. In the face of these memories he is faced with the hard decision of fidelity. In this decision the whole issue of his identity is raised. Is he resourced by the Father for the task? What is his impact on others? Why these feelings of being distraught, disappointed, morose and hurt? His worth and value—John would call it his "glory"—are called into question by the circumstances. Frankly, he is having a bad night.

The bread and the wine are the sign of his determination in the face of potential collapse. His hard decision is expressed in them. Needless to say, his hard decision was not to enter the bread and wine. Some talk about the Eucharist would almost give that impression. By its implicit denial or trivialization of Jesus' humanity and by its consequent downplaying of any negative aspects to the Last Supper, it has little else to say. The bread and wine, however, are insignificant without reference to Jesus' decision to be faithful (classically, to his sacrifice). They are the prop and the humble scenario of his hard choice. In them he concretely and really indicates his desire to give himself to others despite the odds.

But if the Last Supper is seen this way, then what are the implications for our Eucharist? It would be nice to say that we are to sit around and be dutifully impressed by his decision. The Apostles themselves seem to have done this at the Last Supper, listening intently but pushing away from themselves any idea that what was happening to Jesus could happen to them. Like them we are tempted to settle for respectful and awestruck applause of his action. It would be nice, too, simply to take Jesus' decision as a sign, artfully and elaborately arranged for our edification, of God's determined fidelity to us. In this supposition Jesus would be vivid proof that the Father desires, despite all obstacles and despite all legitimate reasons to the contrary, to give himself to humanity, to be its strength and refreshment.

The trouble with this understanding of the matter is twofold. It makes of Jesus' human experience something of a staged morality play, in which the main character is not making a hard-won statement of his own but is miming someone else. Second, there is the risk that we are making the Eucharist into something which feeds our own helplessness and dependency, thus reinforcing a kind of divinely sanctioned infantilism. That Jesus goes through his own drama does not excuse us from going through ours. In fact, he gives us co-responsibility with himself to face the world and to conquer it. He does not feed his Apostles the bread and wine, he shares it with them. He warns them that they will be called upon to do greater things than he did (14:12). And along with this share in Jesus' effective work will come the same hard choices that he had to make to remain faithful to his cause.

It is because the Father is moved by Jesus' fidelity that he promises us support in our hard decisions in the world. On the strength of that promise, we swear great oaths of victory in Jesus' name. The Father has raised Jesus from the dead, and has thereby vindicated Jesus' fidelity. In part, our Eucharist is a jubilant recognition of that truth. But if he has gone on before us, that does not mean that our journey now has built-in shortcuts to it. Our hard decisions are still to be made. They are part, then, of our Eucharist.

These decisions are going to incorporate our real world, the world of today. Hence, our Eucharist will be, as it already is, the meeting place of many currents which eddy about our Gospel decisions: war and world hunger, small successes and large questions, the need for healing, the crazy divisions among Jesus' followers, the heroism, the ordinariness.

This interpretation might seem offensive to those for whom the Eucharist is a "sacred" meal. But the Passover itself which Jesus celebrated was also a sacred meal, in fact the most sacred meal for a pious Jew—only it did not end up looking so sacred. So much was the crisis of his ministry central to that meal that the Passover qualities of it, while suitable to underscore his remarks, were submerged in the drama of his hour. Thus we in our turn cannot sacralize our role in the Eucharist. Nor can we, by our unwillingness to be caught in its glare, tone down the more harrowing dimensions of his experience. We cannot pretend that, because now victorious, he never had his moment of crisis. It would be better to skip the whole thing than to transform the Eucharist into some melodious, aromatic and timeless oasis against the realities either of Jesus' life or of our own.

This eucharistic realism has its rewards. We begin to see some of the attendant aspects of the Last Supper that create the possibility for fidelity and for hard choices. First, there are the presence of friends-in-the-making, of the beginnings of a shared view of things. There was the common background of risks taken in conversation and cooperation. Second, there was the time set aside, the leisure that good decisions need. Third, there was the prayerful setting, where the Father is addressed as a reality-factor in our choices, where complaints can be lodged and the heart exposed. Lastly, there was the simple sharing of bread and wine, the neutrality that eating together requires.

The world needs this very kind of experience today. It needs the Eucharist to discover the kind of choice that really faces it: to love or not to love. In his real presence the world can finally become its real, decisive self.